ONE MINUTE REFERENCE

Word for Windows™ 6

by Elizabeth Mark Keaffaber

alpha books

A Division of Prentice Hall Computer Publishing

201 W. 103rd Street, Indianapolis, Indiana 46290 USA

To Dave, the ultimate Boilermaker fan,
and Matt and Kyle

© **1993 by Alpha Books**

International Standard Book Number: 1-56761-351-9
Library of Congress Catalog Card Number: 93-72392

96 95 94 93   8 7 6 5 4 3 2 1

Interpretation of the printing code: the rightmost number of the first series of numbers is the year of the book's printing; the rightmost number of the second series of numbers is the number of the book's printing. For example, a printing code of 93-1 shows that the first printing of the book occurred in 1993.

Printed in the United States of America

Screen reproductions in this book were created by means of the
program Collage Plus from Inner Media, Inc., Hollis, NH.

Publisher: *Marie Butler-Knight*
Associate Publisher: *Lisa A. Bucki*
Development Editor: *Seta Frantz*
Production Editor: *Linda Hawkins*
Copy Editor: *Audra Gable*
Cover Design: *Jay Corpus*
Interior Design: *Amy Peppler-Adams*
Index: *C. Small*
Production: *Gary Adair, Diana Bigham, Brad Chinn, Tim Cox, Meshell Dinn, Mark Enochs, Howard Jones, Beth Rago, Marc Shecter, Greg Simsic*

Special thanks to Kelly Oliver for ensuring the
technical accuracy of this book.

Contents

Introduction

The *One Minute Reference Word for Windows 6* offers unique help by providing short, clear, step-by-step instructions for when you are in a hurry. This book is designed for the person who:

- Doesn't have time to flip through a large manual.

- Wants only the steps that are necessary to accomplish a task but doesn't want a lot of text.

- Wants no-nonsense instructions to complete a task.

The *One Minute Reference Word for Windows 6* gives easy-to-understand steps for the tasks you need to accomplish quickly.

Conventions Used in This Book

This book offers several design features to make its use as simple as possible. These features include:

- *Alphabetical organization*   Tasks are organized in alphabetical order for quick-and-easy fingertip access of important topics.

- *Keycap column*   All steps are concise, with the keys you need to press or information you need to type to accomplish a task listed to the right of the step.

Keys to press are shown as
keycaps like this... ↵

Information to type is shown
in bold, italic text like this ....***text***

- **(Optional)** Some steps may begin with the
  word **(Optional)**. If you do not wish to use
  this option, press **Enter** to bypass the option.

- Key combinations Key combinations, such
  as **Alt** + **A**, are often used to accomplish a
  task. For example, if you are asked to press
  Alt + **A**, press the **Alt** key and the **A** at the
  same time.

- "OR" If you see an "or" in a step, use the
  method of your choice for that step.

- Some steps will take more than one keypress or
  action. When this is the case, you'll see the
  actions listed vertically. ....**Alt** + **F**
  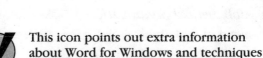

This icon points out extra information
about Word for Windows and techniques
for using Word for Windows features that
you may find valuable.

TIP

This icon gives examples to help you
better understand of how to use the
feature being discussed.

EXAMPLE

Word for Windows Basics

Microsoft Word for Windows 6.0 is a word process-ing package and much more. It lets you revitalize those old documents by formatting them quickly and cleanly. You can create office memos, pictures, letter templates, labels, graphics, and graphs. You can even embed complex mathematical equations with specialized characters into your documents or compile indexes and tables of contents—all without leaving the Word program. Word makes word processing easy: you select menu items rather than typing complex commands. But don't race to lay out your first document just yet! Before you can take advantage of Word, you must learn some basics.

Starting Microsoft Word for Windows

To start Word for Windows 6.0, do the following:

1. At the DOS prompt, type ....**WIN**

2. Press .... ⏎

3. Once you see the Windows Program Manager, open the program group that contains the Microsoft Word icon (usually this is the "Microsoft Office" program group).

4. Double-click on the **Microsoft Word** icon.

5. When the Tip of the Day appears, press .... ⏎

To start Word directly from the DOS prompt,
follow these steps:

1. Start from the DOS prompt
   (C:\>) and type ....**WIN WINWORD**

2. Press .... ⏎

3. When the Tip of the Day
   appears, press .... ⏎

> You must have Windows in order to run the
> Word for Windows program.
>
> **TIP**

The Word for Windows 6.0 title screen appears for
a few moments, and then Word for Windows 6.0
displays an empty document you can begin working
on right away (see Figure 1).

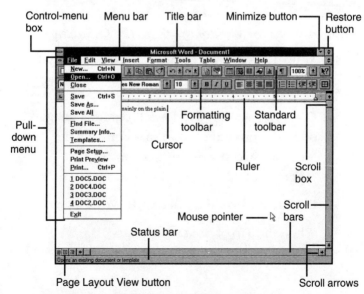

Figure 1   A Word for Windows screen.

Parts of a Word for Windows Screen

The Word for Windows screen contains several distinctive elements that you won't see in DOS. Here's a brief summary:

- *Title bar*   Located along the top of a window or screen, the title bar shows the name of the window or program.

- *Minimize and Maximize buttons*   Located at the upper right corner of a window or screen, these buttons look like a down arrow and up arrow and are used to alter a window's size. The Minimize button shrinks the window to the size of an icon. The Maximize button expands the window to fill the screen. When maximized, a window contains a double-arrow *Restore* button, which returns the window to its original size.

- *Control-menu box*   Located in the upper left corner of a window or screen, the Control-menu box looks like a box with a hyphen in it. When you click on it, a pull-down menu appears, offering size and location controls for the window.

- *Pull-down menu bar*   Located below the title bar, this bar contains a list of the pull-down menus available in the program.

- *Mouse pointer* When you use a mouse, the mouse pointer appears on-screen (usually as an arrow). You control it by moving the mouse.

- *Scroll bars* Scroll bars appear at the bottom or right side of a window, or both. When a window contains more information than it can display, use the *scroll arrows* on each end of the scroll bar to move through the document slowly. Use the *scroll boxes* to move quickly from one screen to the next.

- *Toolbars* When you use a mouse, you can quickly access the toolbars to commonly used commands. The Standard and Formatting toolbars are displayed just below the menu bar.

- *Status bar* Located at the bottom of the window, the status bar provides information about the active document or task you're working on. If you choose a command that may take a few minutes, the status bar displays a message to let you know that the task is under way.

- *Ruler* Displayed at the top of the document window, the ruler allows you to set tab stops and indents for selected paragraphs, adjust column widths, and change page numbers.

- *Page Layout View button*   Located at the left
  end of the horizontal scroll bar, the Page
  Layout View button displays the layout of
  each page in a document as it will look when
  printed. Click on the button to switch a
  document to Page Layout view.

Using a Mouse

*To work efficiently in Word, you should use a
mouse. You press the mouse buttons and move the
mouse to accomplish tasks quickly. The following
list defines the actions you need to be able to
perform with the mouse:*

- *Point* means to move the mouse pointer
  onto the specified item by moving the
  mouse. The tip of the mouse pointer must be
  touching the item.

- *Click on an item* means to move the pointer
  onto the specified item and press the mouse
  button once. Unless specified otherwise, use
  the left mouse button.

- *Double-click on an item* means to move the
  mouse pointer onto the specified item and
  click the left mouse button twice quickly.

- *Drag* means to move the mouse pointer onto
  the specified item, hold down the mouse

button, and move the mouse. Release the
mouse button only when you have placed
the specified item where you want it.

Choosing Menus and Commands

*The pull-down menu bar contains various menus
from which you can select commands. Each Word
application you run has a set of pull-down menus;
Word itself has a set. Each menu name, as well as
the commands on the menu, has an underlined
letter. This is the selection letter you can press to
choose the menu or command with the keyboard.
(Selection letters are indicated in bold in this
book.) To open a menu and choose a command, use
either the mouse steps or the keyboard steps described in the next sections.*

Mouse Steps

1. Click on the menu name on the menu bar.

2. Click on the desired command.

The toolbar buttons are a mouse shortcut
for performing commonly used commands.

Keyboard Steps

1. Choose the menu .... Alt

   + *underlined letter*

2. Choose the command .... *underlined letter*

TIP

Notice that some commands are followed
by key names such as Enter (for the Open
command) or Shift+F2 (for the Copy
command). These are called shortcut keys.
You can use these keys to perform the
specified command without even opening
the menu.

Usually, when you select a command, the
command is performed immediately. However,
there are a few exceptions.

- If the command name appears *gray* (rather
  than black), the command is unavailable at
  the moment, and you cannot choose it.

- If the command name is followed by an
  arrow, selecting that command will cause
  another menu to appear, from which you
  select an option.

- If the command name is followed by an
  ellipsis (three dots), selecting it will cause a
  dialog box to appear. You'll learn about
  dialog boxes in the next section.

Navigating Dialog Boxes

*A dialog box is Windows' way of requesting addi-
tional information. To open a dialog box, choose a
command from one of the menus on the menu bar.
Each dialog box contains one or more of the following elements:*

- *List boxes* display available choices. To activate a list, click inside the list box. You can also press **Tab** to move from option to option. If the entire list is not visible, use the scroll bar to view the items in the list. To select an item from the list, click on it.

- *Drop-down lists* are similar to list boxes, but only one item in the list is shown. To see the rest of the items, click on the down arrow in the right of the box. To select an item from the list, click on it.

- *Text boxes* allow you to type an entry. To activate a text box, click inside it. To edit an existing entry, use the arrow keys to move the cursor and the **Delete** or **Backspace** keys to delete existing characters. Then type your correction.

- *Check boxes* allow you to select one or more items in a group of options. For example, if you are styling text, you may select Bold and Italic to have the text appear in both bold and italic type. Click on a check box to activate it. To deactivate the command, clear the check box by clicking on it again.

- *Option buttons* are like check boxes, but you can select only one option button in a group. Selecting one button *deselects* any option that is already selected. Click on an option button to activate it.

- *Command buttons* execute (or cancel) the command once you have made your selections in the dialog box. To select a command button, click on it.

- *Tabs* are similar to folder tabs; they allow you to see all the available options within the dialog box. For example, the Font dialog box (from the Format menu) has two tabs: the Font tab and the Character spacing tab.

  To close a dialog box, make your decisions and click **OK** or **Cancel**.

Navigating Documents

At any time, you may have one or more documents open and layered on top of one another. These documents are all available, and you can click on the Window menu to switch between them. At the bottom portion of the Window menu are numbered open documents. Click on the document you want to view or press the number. (Only one of the documents is active at a time.)

Selecting and Deselecting Text

You will use these techniques throughout the program to define the portion of the text that you want to move, delete, edit, enhance, overtype, or copy. The text that you select will be highlighted.

Keyboard Steps

Use the arrow keys to position the cursor at the beginning of the text you want to select.

To select	Press...
One character to the right	Shift + →
One character to the left	Shift + ←
The line above	Shift + ↑
The line below	Shift + ↓
Text from the insertion point to the end of the line	Shift + End

TIP

To deselect text, press ↑, ↓, ←, or →.

Exiting Word for Windows 6.0

If you are done and want to exit the program, click on the File menu and click on the Exit command. You will be safely returned to Windows.

Annotation—Insert

Inserts an annotation to remind you of ideas or comments detailing your projects.

EXAMPLE

While preparing a report, let's say you have a sudden brainstorm of new ideas, but you don't want to stop the flow until you finish the topic you're working on. Quickly jot yourself a memo in the document, and you can go back to it later.

Mouse Steps

1. Position the cursor where you want to insert an annotation.

2. Click on the Insert menu.

3. Click on the Annotation command.

4. Type the annotation.

TIP

To keep the annotation pane open and return to the document, click on the document.

5. To return to the document, click on the Close button.

Keyboard Steps

1. Position the cursor where you want to insert an annotation.

2. Pull down the Insert menu .... Alt + I

3. Choose Annotation .... A

TIP

Word for Windows inserts your initials
and numbers the annotation in the pane
in chronological order.

4. Type the annotation.

5. To continue working on your
   document but keep the annotation
   pane open, press F6
   OR
   To close the annotation
   pane, press .... Alt + Shift + C

Annotation—Print

*Prints a list of just the annotations you have
created.*

Mouse Steps

1. Click on the File menu.

2. Click on the Print command.

3. Click on the Print What drop-down list box.

4. Click on the **Annotations** option.

5. To print the annotations only, click on **OK**.

Keyboard Steps

1. Pull down the File menu .... [Alt] + [F]

2. Choose **Print** .... [P]

TIP

The shortcut to steps 1 and 2 is to press **Ctrl+P**.

3. Open the **P**rint What
    drop-down list box .... [Alt] + [P]

4. Select Annotations .... [↑] **or** [↓]

5. To print the annotations only, press .... [←]

Annotation—Print with Document

Prints a document, complete with annotations. The annotations are printed on a separate page at the end of the document text.

Mouse Steps

1. Click on the File menu.

2. Click on the **Print** command.

3. Click on the **O**ptions button.

4. Click on the **A**nnotations check box (located in the Include with Document options box).

5. To close the Options dialog box, click on **OK**.

6. To print a document with the annotations, click on **OK**.

Keyboard Steps

1. Pull down the File menu .... Alt + F
2. Choose Print .... P

TIP

The shortcut to steps 1 and 2 is to press **Ctrl+P**.

3. Select the Options button .... Alt + O
4. From the Include with Document options box, put a check in the Annotations check box .... Alt + A

   Press .... ⏎

5. To print a document with the annotations, press .... ⏎

Annotation—View

Use this command to view the annotations you have inserted in a document. Each annotation has an annotation mark that includes the reviewer's initials and a number. In the annotation pane, the annotation mark appears as normal text. In the document window, the annotation mark appears as hidden text.

Mouse Steps

1. Click on the View menu.

2. Click on the Annotations command.

TIP To keep the annotation pane open and return to the document, click on the document. Or, to close the annotation pane and return to the document, choose the Close button.

Keyboard Steps

1. Pull down the View menu .... Alt + V

2. Choose Annotations .... A

TIP Press **F6** to switch between the annotations pane and the document window.

Annotation Marks—Convert to Text

Converts an annotation to regular body text within your document.

Mouse Steps

1. Open the Annotations pane if it's not already open by clicking on the View menu and selecting Annotations.

2. In the Annotations pane, select the text of the annotation.

3. Click on the **Cut** button on the Standard toolbar.

4. Click the place in the document where you want the text to appear.

5. Click on the **Paste** button on the Standard toolbar.

6. In your document, select the annotation mark for the annotation you just converted to text (see "Select—Text").

7. Press the **Delete** key.

8. **(Optional)** Close the Annotation pane by clicking on the **Close** button.

Keyboard Steps

1. Open the Annotation pane if it's not already open .... Alt + V

    A

2. In the Annotations pane, select the text of the annotation (see "Select— Text") .... Ctrl + Shift + ↑ ↓ ← →

3. Pull down the Edit menu .... Alt + E

4. Choose Cut .... T

Do not select the annotation mark or the paragraph mark at the end of the annotation.

TIP

Ctrl+X is the shortcut for steps 3 and 4.

TIP

5. Switch to the document window F6

6. Position the cursor at the
   insertion point .... ↑ ↓ ← →

7. Pull down the Edit menu .... Alt + E

8. Choose **P**aste .... P

Ctrl+V is the shortcut for steps 7 and 8.

TIP

9. In the document, select the
   annotation mark for the
   annotation you just converted
   to text............. Ctrl + Shift + ↑ ↓ ← →

10. Delete the annotation mark .... Delete

Once you have opened the pane, you can close it by pressing **Alt+Shift+C**.

TIP

Annotation Marks—Display

Annotation marks identify each annotation with a number and your initials.

Mouse Steps

TIP

To display all special characters, including annotation marks, click on the **Show/Hide** (¶) button on the Formatting toolbar.

1. Click on the Tools menu.

2. Click on the Options command.

3. From the Nonprinting Characters options section of the View tab, click on the Hidden Text check box.

4. Click on **OK**.

TIP

To hide the annotation marks, repeat the steps above.

Keyboard Steps

1. Pull down the Tools menu .... Alt + T

2. Choose Options .... O

3. From the Nonprinting Characters options section of the View tab, select the Hidden Text check box ... Alt + I

4. Press ....

TIP

To hide the annotations marks, repeat the steps above.

AutoFormat

After you've typed your document, you can have Word automatically format the text. Word analyzes each paragraph and determines how the paragraph is used within the document—as a heading or an item in a bulleted list. Then a style is applied to improve the document's appearance and provide uniform formatting throughout the document.

Mouse Steps

1. Select the text you want to format (see "Select—Text").

2. Click on the Format menu.

3. Choose AutoFormat.

4. Click on **OK** in the AutoFormat dialog box. Word analyzes the text and applies the styles.

5. Select Review Changes.

6. Use the **Find** buttons to scroll forward or backward to review the changes.

7. **(Optional)** To reject individual changes, click on the **Reject** button.

8. When you are finished, click on **Cancel**.

9. To accept all the changes, click on Accept.
    OR
    To reject all the changes, click on **R**eject All.

Keyboard Steps

1. Select the text you want to format
    (see "Select—Text").

2. Select the Format menu .... `Alt` + `O`

3. Choose AutoFormat .... `A`

4. Choose **OK** .... `↵`
    Word analyzes the text and applies
    the styles.

5. Select Review Changes .... `Alt` + `C`

6. Use the **Find** buttons to scroll through
    the document and review the formatting
    changes .... `Alt` + `F` and `Alt` + `I`

7. **(Optional)** To reject individual
    changes, choose the **R**eject
    button .... `Alt` + `R`

8. When you are finished, choose
    Cancel .... `Tab`
    `↵`

9. To accept all the changes, select
    Accept .... `Alt` + `A`
    OR

To reject all the changes,

select **Reject All** .... Alt + R

AutoText Entry—Create

Allows you to store items for reuse and to assign, revise, reassign, and delete AutoText entries.

EXAMPLE

If you find yourself typing the same thing over and over again, stop typing. By storing those items as an AutoText entry, you eliminate the need to reinvent the wheel. Some examples of items you can store are your address, copyright information, a company logo, standard clauses, and so on.

TIP

If you are interested in storing information from various documents, try storing them in the Spike (see "Spike—Collect Text or Graphics" and "Spike—Insert").

Mouse Steps

1. Select the text or graphic to specify as AutoText.

2. Click on the **Edit** menu.

3. Click on the AutoText command.

A shortcut to steps 2 and 3 is to press the **AutoText** button on the Standard toolbar.

4. Click on a preexisting entry you want to reassign, or type a name for the new AutoText entry in the Name text box using up to 31 characters.

To delete an AutoText entry, click on the entry in the **Name** list box and click on the **Delete** button.

5. To return to the document and store text or graphics as an AutoText entry, click on the Add button.

6. If you want to cancel the action, click on the **Cancel** button.

If you are reassigning an AutoText entry, a dialog box will ask, "Do you want to redefine the AutoText entry?" Answer **Yes**, **No**, or **Help**.

Keyboard Steps

1. Select the text or graphic to specify as AutoText.

2. Pull down the Edit menu ....[Alt] + [E]

3. Choose AutoText X

4. Choose a preexisting entry you
   want to reassign .... ↑ **or** ↓
   OR
   Type a name using up to 31
   characters for the new AutoText
   entry in the Name text box .... *name*

TIP

To delete an AutoText entry, highlight the
entry in the **Name** list box and choose
Delete by pressing **Alt+D**.

5. To return to the document and
   store text or graphics as an
   AutoText entry, press Add .... Alt **+** A
   OR
   If you want to cancel the action,
   press **Escape**
   or tab to **Cancel** .... Esc **or** Tab
                                                        ↵

TIP

If you are reassigning an AutoText entry, a
dialog box will ask, "Do you want to
redefine the AutoText entry?" Answer **Yes**
(press **Y**), No (press **N**), or Help (press **H**).

AutoText Entry—Insert

Inserts the contents of the AutoText entry into a document. Word for Windows allows you to insert the entry as you typed it, or stripped of the formats you typed, in which case it then picks up the format of the text around it.

Mouse Steps

1. Position the cursor where you want to insert the contents of the AutoText entry.

2. Click on the **Edit** menu.

3. Click on the AutoText command.

TIP To insert AutoText quickly, highlight the space where you want to insert an AutoText entry and press the **AutoText** button on the Standard toolbar.

4. Click on the entry you want to insert in the document.

5. To insert the contents of the AutoText entry, click on the **Insert** button.

Keyboard Steps

1. Position the cursor where you want to insert the contents of the AutoText entry.

2. Pull down the **Edit** menu ....**Alt** + **E**

3. Choose the AutoText command ....**X**

4. Select the entry you want to insert
   in the document .... ⬆ or ⬇

5. Press .... ⏎

AutoText Entry—Print

*Prints an alphabetical list of all the AutoText
entries you have created.*

Mouse Steps

1. Click on the **File** menu.

2. Click on the **Print** command.

3. From the **Print** What drop-down list box, click
   on **AutoText Entries**.

4. To print the list of AutoText entries in alphabetical order, click **OK**.

Keyboard Steps

1. Open the **File** menu .... Alt + F

2. Choose **Print** .... P

Skip steps 1 and 2 by pressing **Ctrl+P**.

TIP

3. From the **Print** What drop-down
   list box, choose AutoText Entries .... Alt + P
   ⬆ or ⬇

4. To print the list of AutoText entries
    in alphabetical order, press ....

Bookmark—Insert

*Inserts bookmarks to mark selected text, graphics,
tables, and other items. Bookmarks are useful for
jumping to a specific location in a document,
marking an item so that you can refer to it in a
cross-reference, or marking a range of pages for an
index entry.*

Mouse Steps

1. Position the cursor where you want to mark
    the text.

2. Click on the **Edit** menu.

3. Choose the **Bookmark** command.

4. Type the bookmark name in the text box.

5. To insert the bookmark, click on **Add.**

Keyboard Steps

1. Position the cursor where you
    want to mark the text.

2. Pull down the **Edit** menu .... `Alt` + `E`

3. Choose **Bookmark** .... `B`

TIP

Pressing **Ctrl+Shift+F5** is the shortcut for steps 1 and 2.

4. Type the bookmark name in the text box.

5. To insert the bookmark, press ....

Bookmark—Locate

Quickly moves the cursor to the bookmark's location in the document.

Mouse Steps

1. Open the **Edit** menu.

2. Select **Bookmark**.

3. Select the **Location** option button to sort through the bookmark names.

4. Select the bookmark name you want to locate.

5. Choose the **Go To** button. Word moves the cursor to the bookmark.

6. When you are finished, press the **Close** button.

Keyboard Steps

1. Open the **Edit** menu .... Alt + E

2. Choose **Bookmark** .... B

3. Select the Location option button
   to sort through the bookmark
   names .... `Alt` + `L`

4. Select the bookmark name you
   want to locate .... `Alt` + `B`
                                             `↑` or `↓`

5. Choose the Go To button .... `G`
                                             `⏎`

   Word moves the cursor to the
   bookmark.

6. When you are finished, press .... `⏎`

Border—Add

Encloses text, graphics, figures, table cells, or tables with a border.

Mouse Steps

1. Select the text, graphic, figure, table cell, or
   table to enclose with a border.

2. Click on the Format menu.

3. Click on the Borders and Shading command.

4. From the Presets section, click on the Box
   option.

Select the **Borders** button from the Formatting toolbar, to apply commonly used border effects and shading.

5. Click on a line style from the Style list box.

6. To add a border, click on **OK**.

To delete a border, click on **None** from the Presets section or press **Alt+N**.

Keyboard Steps

1. Select the text, graphic, figure, table cell, or table you want to enclose with a border.

2. Pull down the Format menu .... **Alt** + **O**

3. Choose **B**orders and Shading .... **B**

4. From the Presets section, select Box .... **X**

5. Select a line style from the Style options .... **Alt** + **Y**

   ↑ or **↓**

6. To add a border, press .... **↵**

Bullet—Add

Adds bullets (symbols) to mark items in para-graphs. Used for itemized lists.

Mouse Steps

TIP

You can also click on the **Bullets** button on the Formatting toolbar.

1. Select the text to which you want to add bullets.

2. Click on the Format menu.

3. Click on the Bullets and Numbering com-mand.

4. Click on the bullet style you want from the Bulleted tab.

5. **(Optional)** Choose Modify to change the bullet character or the bullet position.

6. To add the bullet to the text, click on **OK**.

Keyboard Steps

1. Select the text to which you want to add bullets.

2. Pull down the Format menu .... <kbd>Alt</kbd> + <kbd>O</kbd>

3. Choose Bullets and Numbering .... <kbd>N</kbd>

4. Choose the bullet style you
   want .... ⬆️ ⬇️ ⬅️ ➡️

5. **(Optional)** To change the bullet
   character or bullet position,
   choose **M**odify .... Alt + M

6. To add the bullet to the text, press .... ⏎

Bullet—Delete

Deletes the bullets from a document.

Mouse Steps

1. Select the text that contains the bullet(s) you
   want to delete.

2. Click on the Format menu.

3. Click on the Bullets and Numbering command.

4. To remove the hanging indent, click the
   Hanging Indent check box.

TIP A quick way to create a bulleted list is to
select the paragraphs you want to include
and then click on the **Bullets** button on
the Formatting toolbar. (You can also use
this method to remove bullets.)

5. To delete the bullet, click on the **Remove**
   button.

Keyboard Steps

1. Select the text that contains the bullet(s) you want to delete.

2. Pull down the Format menu .... `Alt` + `O`

3. Choose Bullets and Numbering .... `N`

4. To remove the hanging indent, clear the Hanging Indent check box... `Alt` + `A`

5. To delete the bullet, choose Remove .... `Alt` + `R`

Calculations

See "Table—Calculations."

Captions—Add

Captions label, explain, or point out areas of interest in selected text, an illustration, table, equation, graph, or other item within a document.

Mouse Steps

1. Select the item to which you want to add a caption.

2. Select the Insert menu.

3. Choose Caption. Word displays the label and item number in the Caption box.

4. **(Optional)** To add text, type in the Caption box.

5. **(Optional)** To add a new label, choose the
    New Label button, type the name, and choose
    OK.

6. **(Optional)** To select a position for the cap-
    tion, select **Below Selected Item** or **Above
    Selected Item** in the Position box.

7. **(Optional)** To change the number format,
    click on the Numbering button, select the
    number, and then choose **OK**.

8. Choose **OK**.

Keyboard Steps

1. Select the item to which you want
    to add a caption.

2. Open the Insert menu .... $\boxed{\text{Alt}}$ + $\boxed{\text{I}}$

3. Choose Caption .... $\boxed{\text{I}}$
    Word displays the label and item
    number in the Caption box.

4. **(Optional)** To add text, type in
    the Caption box.. $\boxed{\text{C}}$
    text

5. **(Optional)** To add a new label,
    choose the New Label button, type
    the name, and choose **OK**............................ $\boxed{\text{N}}$
    text
    $\boxed{\leftarrow}$

6. **(Optional)** To select a position for the caption, select Below Selected Item or Above Selected Item in the **P**osition box .... [P]

[↑] **or** [↓]

7. **(Optional)** To change the number format, choose the **N**umbering button, select the number, and then choose **OK** .... [N]

[↑] **or** [↓]

[↵]

8. Choose **OK** .... [↵]

Character Style

See "Format—Character."

Close—Document/File

Closes a document without quitting Word.

Mouse Steps

1. Pull down the **F**ile menu.

2. Choose **C**lose.

3. Word will ask you if you want to save the changes before closing. Answer **Y**es or **N**o. If you choose **Y**es but have not named the document, Word displays the Save As dialog box. (See "Save As—Document/File.")

4. Type the document name and click **OK**.

TIP

You can double-click on the Control-menu box in the upper left corner of the document window to close a document.

Keyboard Steps

1. Open the File menu ....$\boxed{\text{Alt}}$ + $\boxed{\text{F}}$

2. Choose Close ....$\boxed{\text{C}}$

3. Word will ask you if you want to save the changes before closing. Answer **Yes** or **No**. If you choose Yes but have not named the document, Word displays the Save As dialog box ....$\boxed{\text{Y}}$ or $\boxed{\text{N}}$

4. Type the document name ....*text*

5. Press ....$\boxed{\text{←}}$

Columns—Newspaper

Creates columns where the page is divided into equal sections. Text begins in the upper left column. When the first column is full, the text wraps up to the top of the next column.

Mouse Steps

TIP

To quickly convert text to Newspaper columns, click on the **Columns** button on the Standard toolbar. To select the number of columns you prefer, press the left mouse button and drag to the right as you highlight the number of columns.

1. Position the cursor where you want to begin the columns or highlight the specific text you want put into column format.

2. Choose the Format menu.

3. Select the Columns command.

4. In the Number of Columns text box, type a number.

5. Click on the Apply To options box and select how much of the document you want to change.

6. To create columns, click **OK**.

7. **(Optional)** To view the newspaper columns, click on the **Page Layout View** button in the horizontal scroll bar.

Keyboard Steps

1. Position the cursor where you want to begin the columns or highlight the specific text you want put into a column format.

2. Pull down the Format menu ....|Alt| + |O|

3. Choose Columns ....|C|

4. Type a number in the **Number** of
columns text box..**#**

5. Activate the **A**pply To
options box.................................|Alt| + |A|

6. Choose an option ....|↑| or |↓|

7. To create columns, press ....|↵|

8. (**Optional**) To view the newspaper
columns, pull down the **V**iew
menu and choose **P**age Layout ....|Alt| + |V|

|P|

Copy—Document/File

*Copies files to another location while keeping the
original in the same location.*

Mouse Steps

1. Click on the File menu.

2. Click on Find File.

3. In the Find File dialog box, select the file or
files you want to copy.

4. Choose the **C**ommands button.

5. Choose **C**opy.

6. In the **Directories** and **Drives** boxes, select the location to which you want to copy your files.

7. Select the **OK** button.

Keyboard Steps

1. Open the File menu .... Alt + F

2. Choose Find File .... F

3. In the Find File dialog box, select the file or files you want to copy .... ↑ or ↓

4. Choose the Commands button .... Alt + C

5. Select Copy C

6. In the **Directories** and **Drives** boxes, select the location to which you want to copy the files .... ↑ or ↓

7. Press .... ↵

Copy—Text

Copies selected text to the Windows Clipboard.

Mouse Steps—To Clipboard

1. Select the text you want to copy.

TIP

To copy a selection of text to the Clipboard, click the **Copy** button on the Standard toolbar.

2. Click on the **Edit** menu.

3. Click on the **Copy** command.

Drag and Drop—No Clipboard

TIP

You can only drag and drop text using the mouse.

1. Select the text you want to copy.

2. Position the mouse pointer anywhere on the selected text.

3. Press and hold **Ctrl**.

4. Hold down the left mouse button.

5. Drag the pointer to the desired location.

Keyboard Steps

1. Select the text you want to copy (see "Select—Text").

2. Pull down the **Edit** menu ....Alt + E

3. Choose **Copy** C

TIP

You can use the shortcut key combination, **Ctrl+C**, to quickly copy text to the Clipboard.

Create New Document

See "New Document—Create."

Cross-Reference—Create

Creates a cross-reference. A cross-reference tells readers where additional information is located in the same document or another document.

Mouse Steps

1. In the document, type the text that begins the cross-reference (for example, *See also*).

2. Open the Insert menu.

3. Choose Cross-reference.

4. In the Reference Type box, select the type of item.

5. In the Insert Reference To box, select the information you want to insert in the document.

6. In the For Which Caption box, select the specific item to which you want to refer.

7. Choose the Insert button. The dialog box stays open so that you can add additional information.

8. Choose **Close**.

Keyboard Steps

1. In the document, type the text that begins the cross-reference (for example, *See also*).

2. Open the Insert menu .... [Alt] + [I]

3. Choose Cross-reference .... [R]

4. In the Reference Type box, select the type of item .... [↑] or [↓]

5. In the Insert Reference To box, select the information you want to insert in the document .... [Alt] + [R]
   [↑] or [↓]

6. In the For Which Caption box, select the specific item to which you want to refer .... [Alt] + [W]
   [↑] or [↓]

7. Choose the Insert button .... [Alt] + [I]
   The dialog box stays open so that you can add additional information.

8. Press .... [↵]

Cross-Reference—Update

You can manually update the fields containing cross-references.

Mouse Step

1. Position the insertion point on the field you want to update.

2. Click on the right mouse button.

3. Choose **Update Field** from the menu.

4. Type in the new reference number.

Keyboard Steps

1. Position the insertion point in the field you want to update .... ↑ ↓ ← →

2. Press F9

3. Type in the new reference number .... #

Customize Toolbar

See "Toolbar—Customize."

Data Source—Adding Information

Type information into the data source under your field name headings. See also "Mail Merge—Merge with Data Source" and "Data Source—Create."

TIP

Be sure every record has the same number of fields, even if you have to leave some blank.

Mouse Steps

1. Select the Tools menu.

2. Choose Mail Merge.

3. Under Data Source, choose the Edit button.

4. Click on the data source.

5. Type the information in each field box, pressing **Enter** to go to the next field.

6. Choose the Add New button to start a new record.

7. Click **OK** when you are finished.

Keyboard Steps

1. Select the Tools menu .... `Alt` + `T`

2. Choose Mail Merge .... `R`

3. Under Data Source, choose the
   Edit button .... `Alt` + `D`

4. Select the data source .... `↑` **or** `↓`
   `↵`

5. Type the information in each field
   box .... *text*
   `↵`

6. Choose the Add New button to
   start the new record .... `Alt` + `A`

7. When you are finished, choose OK .... `Tab`
   `↵`

Data Source—Create

A data source is one of the files you must create when you are merging two documents. It contains the variable information, such as names, numbers, and addresses.

EXAMPLE

You can mail a form letter using the data source. Merge the data source, which contains all the personal information, with the main document file, which contains all the fixed information to complete this task.

Mouse Steps

1. Click on the Tools menu.

2. Choose Mail Merge.

3. In the Mail Merge Helper dialog box, select Get Data.

4. Choose Create Data Source.

5. In the Field Names In Header Row box, Word lists field names. Scroll to see all the names.

6. Select one of the following options:

Delete a Field Name	Select the field name and choose the Remove Field Name button.
Add Field Name	Type a new field name in the Field

	Name box and choose Add Field Name.
Change Order of Field Name	Select a field name and then click the up or down arrows until the name is in the position.

7. Choose **OK**.

8. Type a name for the new document in the File Name box and press **Enter**.

9. Word displays a message asking you whether you want to edit the data source or main document. Choose the Edit **D**ata Source button.

10. Type in the information that varies and click OK when you are finished. (See "Data Source—Adding Information.")

Keyboard Steps

1. Pull down the Tools menu .... Alt + T

2. Choose Mail Me**r**ge .... R

3. In the Mail Merge Helper dialog box, select **G**et Data .... Alt + G

4. Choose **C**reate Data Source C

5. Select the Field **N**ames In Header Row box .... Alt + N
   Word lists the field names.
   Scroll to see all the names .... ↑ or ↓

6. Select one of the following options:

Delete a Field Name	Select a field name and choose the **R**emove Field Name button.
Add a Field Name	Type a new field name in the **F**ield Name box and choose **A**dd Field Name button.
Change Order of Field Names	Select a field name and use the arrow keys to highlight the name.

7. Choose **OK** .... ↵

8. Type a name for the new document in the File **N**ame box .... *text*

   ↵

9. Word displays a message asking you whether you want to edit the data source or the main document. Choose the Edit **D**ata Source button .... D

10. Type in the information that varies .... *text*

11. When you are finished, press .... ↵

Date and Time

Automatically inserts any combination of the date and time into the document.

EXAMPLE

If you revise the same documents over and over, using this command will help you recognize which one is the most recent copy. You can use the Insert Date and Time command when writing resumes and cover letters to make sure you send the revised copy to your potential employer.

TIP

If the wrong date or time keeps showing up in your documents, you must correct the computer's clock.

Mouse Steps

1. Position the cursor where you want to insert the date or the time.

2. Click on the Insert menu.

3. Click on the Date and Time command.

4. Click on the items you want to appear on your document.

5. To accept your current selection, click on **OK**.

Keyboard Steps

1. Position the cursor where you want to insert the date or the time.

2. Pull down the Insert menu ....`Alt` + `I`

3. Choose Date and Time.................................`T`

4. Select the item that you want to appear on your document.................`↑` or `↓`

5. To accept current choices, press ....`⏎`

TIP

You can use this shortcut for inserting the date or the time.

To insert	Format	Press
Date	00/00/	`Alt` + `Shift` + `D`
Time	00:00 am or pm (in hours and minutes)	`Alt` + `Shift` + `T`

Default—Change Character Formatting

Changes the font, font size, and other formats that are preset by Word.

Mouse Steps

1. Select the Format menu.

2. Choose Font.

3. To set a new font, type or select a font in the Font box.
    OR
    To set a new font size, type or select the size in the Size box.

4. Choose the Default button.

5. To confirm changes, choose **Yes**.

Keyboard Steps

1. Select the Format menu .... `Alt` + `O`

2. Choose Font .... `F`

3. To set a new font, type or select a
    font in the Font box .... `Alt` + `F`
    text

    OR
    To set a new font size, type or
    select the size in the Size box.......... `Alt` + `S`
    text

4. Choose the Default button.............. `Alt` + `D`

5. To confirm changes, choose **Yes** .... `Y`

Delete—Document/File

Removes an unwanted document from your disk drive.

TIP

Before you delete any document from your hard drive, make a copy of it on a floppy disk. If you find out later that you need the document, it will be easy to retrieve it from the floppy disk.

Mouse Steps

1. Click on the File menu.

2. Choose Find File.

3. Highlight the file or files you want to delete.

4. Click on the Commands button and press **Enter**.

5. Select **Delete**.

6. When Word asks if you want to delete the file, click on **Yes**.

Keyboard Steps

1. Pull down the File menu .... **Alt** + **F**

2. Choose Find File .... **F**

3. Highlight the file or files you want to delete .... **↑** or **↓**

4. Select the Commands button .... **Alt** + **C**

5. Select **Delete** .... D

6. When Word asks if you want to
   delete the file, answer Yes .... ←┘

Delete—Text

Deletes text by letter, word, sentence, line, para-graph, block, or entire document.

TIP

Anytime you plan to delete anything or make major changes to a document, it's a good idea to save the document under a different name using the Save **As** com-mand (see "Save As—Document/File"). This gives you the option of going back to the original document at any time.

Mouse Steps

1. Highlight the item of your choice (see "Select—Text").

2. Press **Delete**.

Keyboard Steps

Delete the item of your choice using these methods:

Item	Instruction	Press
Character	Position the cursor to the left of the character.	Delete

Word	Position cursor to the right of the word.	`Ctrl` + `Back`
Sentence	Position cursor to the left of the first word; hold down **Shift** and use the →key to highlight the whole sentence.	`Delete`
Line	Position cursor to the left of the line; hold down **Shift** and press **End**.	`Delete`
Paragraph or Block	Follow the instructions for deleting a line, keep holding down **Shift**, and use the ↓to finish selecting the block or paragraph.	`Delete`
Entire document	Highlight the whole. document (press **Ctrl+5** on the numeric keypad, with NumLock turned on).	`Delete`

TIP

To delete using the Backspace key, position your cursor to the right of the item you want to delete.

Document

*See "Close—Document/File," "Create—New
Document," "Delete—Document/File," "Open—
Document/File," "Preview—Document/File,"
"Print—Document/File," "Save—Document/File,"
"Save As—Document/File," or "View—Document."*

Drag and Drop

See "Copy—Text."

Drop Caps—Create

*Creates a large initial or dropped capital letter.
Drop caps are oversized letters that dip below the
baseline into the lines of text below, bumping the
text below to the right. They are often used to start
a new chapter or an article.*

Mouse Steps

1. Select the text.

2. Open the Format menu.

3. Choose Drop Cap.

4. Under Position, select Dropped or In Margin.

5. In the Font box, type or select the font.

6. In the Lines to Drop box, type or select the
   height of the letter.

7. In the Distance from Text box, type or select

the amount of space between the letter and the following text.

8. Choose **OK**.

9. If you are not in Page Layout view, Word will ask if you want to switch. Choose **Yes**.

Keyboard Steps

1. Select the text.

2. Open the Format menu .... `Alt` + `O`

3. Choose **Drop Cap** .... `D`

4. Under Position, select **Dropped** or In Margin .... `Alt` + `D` or `Alt` + `M`

5. In the Font box, type or select the font .... `Alt` + `F`

 `↑` or `↓`

6. In the Lines to Drop box, type or select the height of the letter .... `Alt` + `L`

 `↑` or `↓`

7. In the Distance from Text box, type or select the amount of space between the letter and the following text .... `Alt` + `X`

 `↑` or `↓`

8. Choose .... `⏎`

Envelopes—Print

Use this feature to print addresses on envelopes.

Mouse Steps

1. Within the document, highlight the address you want on the envelope.

2. Click on the Tools menu.

3. Click on the Envelopes and Labels command.

4. **(Optional)** To include a return address, click inside the **R**eturn Address box. Type a return address in the box.

5. To select the size of an envelope, click on the envelope in the Preview section and then use the Envelope **S**ize drop-down list box.

6. Click on the **P**rint button.

Keyboard Steps

1. Within the document, highlight the address you want to print on the envelope ....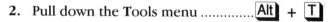

2. Pull down the Tools menu ....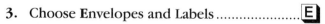

3. Choose Envelopes and Labels .... E

The address you selected appears in the Delivery Address text box on the Envelopes tab of the Envelopes and Labels dialog box. Edit if necessary.

4. **(Optional)** Type a return address
    in the **R**eturn Address text box .... Alt + R

    text

TIP

If you don't want to include a return
address, choose **O**mit on the Envelopes
tab by pressing **Alt+M**.

5. To set options, choose the
    Options button .... Alt + O

6. Choose a size from the
    Envelope **S**ize drop-down
    list box .... Alt + S

    ↑ or ↓

7. Select OK .... ↵

8. To print the envelope, select the
    Print button .... Alt + P

File—Select Multiple in Find File

*Executes commands, such as Open, Print, Sum-
mary, Search, Delete, Copy, Options, and Close, to
one file or a group of files.*

Mouse Steps

1. Click on the **F**ile menu.
2. Click on the Find File command.

3. Select the files using one of these methods:

    If you want to open more than one file in consecutive order, hold down **Shift** as you click on the files.

    If you want to open more than one file *not* in consecutive order, hold down **Ctrl** as you click on the files.

Keyboard Steps

1. Pull down the File menu .... Alt + F
2. Choose Find File .... F
3. Turn on Select mode .... Shift + F8
4. Highlight the first file .... ↑ or ↓
5. Press the **Spacebar** to select each file .... Space

TIP   If you select the wrong file, highlight it and press the **Spacebar** again. The Spacebar acts as a toggle, turning it on or off.

6. When you are finished, turn off Select mode .... Shift + F8

File Format—Convert

Converts a file to and from a different format.

Mouse Steps

1. Click on the File menu.

2. Select Save As.

3. Select the file you want to convert (see also "Open—File").

4. Click on Save As Type.

5. Scroll through the list and select an option.

6. Click **OK**.

Word only recognizes files that have the .DOC extension. If it doesn't accept the name as it is, you may need to rename the file before you convert it.

Keyboard Steps

1. Pull down the File menu .... `Alt` + `F`

2. Select Save As .... `A`

3. Select the file to be converted (see also "Open—File").

4. Click on Save As Type................................. `T`

5. Scroll through the list and select an option .... `↓` or `↑`

Word only recognizes files that have the .DOC extension. If it doesn't accept the name as it is, you may need to rename the file before converting it.

6. To convert the file, press .... ⏎

Find—Document/File

Searches for and finds specified files.

Mouse Steps

1. Click on the File menu.

2. Click on Find File.

3. From the command buttons at the bottom of your screen, click on the Search option.

4. Click in the File Name text box.

5. Type the file name.

EXAMPLE To find all files under one directory, type *.*. To find a group of files, such as all the document files, you would type *.doc. To find a smaller subgroup, such as all files that start with LET, type **LET?????.doc**. The asterisk and the question mark are wild-card characters.

6. Begin the search by clicking on **OK**.

Keyboard Steps

1. Pull down the File menu .... [Alt] + [F]

2. Choose Find File .... [F]

3. From the command buttons at the bottom of your screen, choose Search .... [Alt] + [S]

4. Activate the File Name text box ....

5. Type the file name.

> Word will not accept a hyphen (–) or a
> space as a character. But it will accept an
> asterisk (*) and a question mark (?).
>
> **TIP**

6. Begin the search by choosing OK .... ⏎

Find and Replace—Text

*Searches a document for specified text or format-
ting and replaces it.*

Mouse Steps

1. Position the cursor at the location you want to
   start the search.

2. Click on the Edit menu.

3. Click on the Replace command.

> To simply find text or formats, use the
> Find command instead of the Replace
> command.
>
> **TIP**

4. To search for text:
   Type the text you want to find in the Find
   What text box.

Click on the Replace With text box and type the text you want to replace.

Click on any of the following options, and then skip to step 7:

Match **C**ase (uppercase/lowercase)

Find **W**hole Words Only

Use Pattern **M**atching (special search)

Sounds **L**ike

5. To search for character formats:
Select F**ormat** and then click on **F**ont.
Click on the character format(s) you want to find.
Click **OK**.
Click on the Replace With text box.
Select the F**ormat** button and click on **F**ont.
Click on a different character format(s).
Click **OK**.
Then skip to step 7.

6. To search for paragraph formats:
Select F**ormat** and click on the **P**aragraph button.
Click on the paragraph format(s) you want to find.
Click **OK**.
Click on the Replace With text box.
Select F**ormat**, and then click on the **P**aragraph button.
Click on a different paragraph format(s).
Click **OK**.

7. Click on the Find Next button.

8. To replace the item and then find the next occurrence, click on the Replace button. To replace all occurrences, click on the Replace All option.
To stop the search and replace operation, click on **Close**.

9. After Word finishes searching the document, a dialog box asks if you want to continue searching from the top of the document. (If you forgot to start at the beginning, this might be helpful.) Answer this question by clicking on Yes or No.

Keyboard Steps

1. Position the cursor at the location you want to start the search.

2. Pull down the Edit menu ....**Alt** + **E**

3. Choose Replace ....**E**

To simply find text or formatting, use the Find command instead of the Replace command.

TIP

4. To search for text:
Type the text you want to find in the Find What text box ....***text***

Activate the Replace With
text box ....⌨Alt + ⌨P
Type the replacement text ....*text*
Choose one of the following
options, and then skip to step 7:

Match Case
(uppercase/lowercase) ....⌨Alt + ⌨C

Find Whole Words Only ....⌨Alt + ⌨W

Use Pattern Matching
(special search) ....⌨Alt + ⌨M

Sounds Like ....⌨Alt + ⌨L

5. To search for character formats:
   Select Format..................................⌨Alt + ⌨O
   Choose Font ....⌨F
   Choose the character format(s)
   you want to find ....⌨Alt + *underlined letter*
                                            ⌨↑ or ⌨↓
                                            ⌨↵

   Activate the Replace With
   text box ....⌨Alt + ⌨P
   Select Format ....⌨Alt + ⌨O
   Choose Font ....⌨F
   Choose a font
   format(s) ....⌨Alt + *underlined letter*
                                            ⌨↑ or ⌨↓
   Press ....⌨↵

   Skip to step 7.

6. To search for paragraph formats:
   Select F**ormat** .... `Alt` + `O`
   Choose **P**aragraph .... `P`
   Choose the paragraph format(s)
   you want to find .... `Alt` + *underlined letter*
   `↑` or `↓`
   `↵`

   Activate the Re**p**lace With
   text box .... `Alt` + `P`
   Select F**ormat** .... `Alt` + `O`
   Choose **P**aragraph .... `P`
   Choose a different paragraph
   format(s) .... `Alt` + *underlined letter*
   `↑` or `↓`
   Press .... `↵`

7. Choose Find Next .... `Alt` + `F`

8. To replace the item and then find
   the next occurrence, choose
   Replace .... `Alt` + `R`
   To replace all occurrences,
   choose Replace **A**ll........................... `Alt` + `A`
   To stop the search and replace
   operation, press .... `Esc`

9. After Word finishes searching the
   document, a dialog box asks if you
   want to continue searching from
   the top of the document. (If you
   forgot to start the search at the

beginning of the document, this
might be helpful.) Answer by
choosing **Yes** or **No**............................[Y] or [N]

Footnotes

*Footnotes explain, comment on, or provide refer-
ences for the text in a document. Use this feature to
add footnotes to the bottom or top of a page and/or
at the end of the text page, section, or document.*

Mouse Steps

1. Position the cursor in the document where
    you want to put the footnote number.

2. Click on the **Insert** menu.

3. Click on the **Footnote** command.

4. You can automatically number the footnotes
    by clicking on **AutoNumber**.

TIP

To create customized footnotes, click on
the **Custom Mark** option button in the
Footnote and Endnote dialog box. In the
text box, type in an original mark using up
to 10 characters.

5. Specify other footnote options by clicking on
    the **Options** button.

6. **(Optional)** Choose from the following
    options:

Option	Description
Place At	Changes the placement of footnotes on the page: bottom of page, beneath text, or end of section or document.
Number Format	Changes the number format of footnotes: 1, 2, 3; A, B, C; or symbols.
Start At	Selects the number sequence to start footnotes.
Numbering	Changes the numbering sequence of footnotes: Continuous, Restart Each Section, or Restart Each Page.

7. Click on **OK**.

8. Click on **OK**.

9. After Word for Windows inserts the footnote reference mark in the Footnotes pane, type in the text of the footnote.

10. To close the Footnotes pane, click on **Close**.

To keep the Footnotes pane open as you work on your document, click on the document window.

TIP

Keyboard Steps

1. Position the cursor in the document where you want to put the footnote number.

2. Pull down the Insert menu ....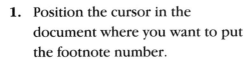

3. Choose Footnote ....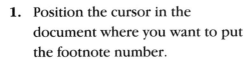

4. You can automatically number the footnotes by selecting AutoNumber ....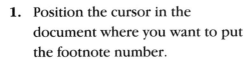

EXAMPLE

To create customized footnotes, activate the **Custom Mark** option button (press **Alt+C**). In the text box, type in an original mark using up to 10 characters.

5. Specify other footnotes options by choosing the Options button ....

6. Specify the position of the footnotes by activating the **P**lace At list box ....
   Then choose from these options:

Option	Description
Place At	Changes the placement of footnotes on the page: bottom of page, beneath text, or end of section or document.
Number Format	Changes the number format of footnotes: 1, 2, 3; A, B, C; or symbols.

| Start **At** | Selects the number sequence to start footnotes. |
| Numbering | Changes the numbering sequence of footnotes: Continuous, Restart Each Section, or Restart Each Page. |

7. Choose **OK** twice .... ⏎
   ⏎

8. After Word for Windows inserts the footnote reference mark in the Footnotes pane, type in the text of the footnote .... ***text***

9. To switch back to the document, press F6

10. To close the pane altogether, press .... Shift + Alt + C

Format—Character

Enhances text and changes the appearance of single letters, sentences, paragraphs, or entire documents. You can emphasize special letters, words, or paragraphs by using format features such as bold, italic, or underline. The following table displays the formatting options available.

Option	Description
Font	Specifies character style.
Font Style	Includes Regular, Bold, Italic, or Bold Italic.
Size	Specifies character size.
Underline	Includes None, Single, Double, Dotted, or Words Only.
Color	Specifies color of character on-screen. Choose from 16 colors.
Character Spacing tab	Increases or decreases the amount of space after a selected character by the amount you specify.
Effects	Includes Hidden, Small caps, All Caps, Strikethrough, Super-script, and Subscript.

Mouse Steps

1. Select the text to format.

2. Click on the Format menu.

3. Click on the Font command.

4. Choose from the character format options in the table above. The effects you have assigned

to the text will be displayed in the Preview box.

5. Click on **OK**.

Keyboard Steps

1. Select the text to format.

2. Pull down the Format menu .... 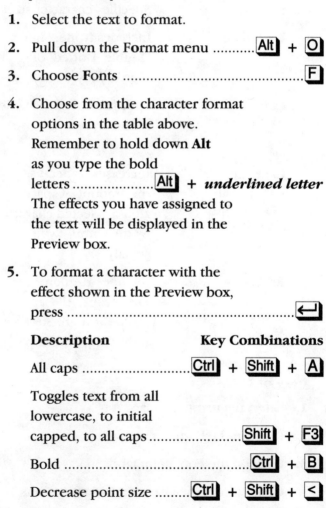 Alt + O

3. Choose Fonts .... F

4. Choose from the character format options in the table above. Remember to hold down **Alt** as you type the bold letters .... Alt + *underlined letter* The effects you have assigned to the text will be displayed in the Preview box.

5. To format a character with the effect shown in the Preview box, press .... ⏎

Description	Key Combinations
All caps	Ctrl + Shift + A
Toggles text from all lowercase, to initial capped, to all caps	Shift + F3
Bold	Ctrl + B
Decrease point size	Ctrl + Shift + <

Double underline .... `Ctrl` + `Shift` + `D`

Font .... `Ctrl` + `Shift` + `F`

Hidden text .... `Ctrl` + `Shift` + `H`

Italic .... `Ctrl` + `I`

Type point size in box ..... `Ctrl` + `Shift` + `P`

Remove character
formatting .... `Ctrl` + `Shift` + `Z`

Small caps .... `Ctrl` + `Shift` + `K`

Subscript .... `Ctrl` + `=`

Superscript .... `Ctrl` + `Shift` + `=`

Underline .... `Ctrl` + `U`

Word underline .... `Ctrl` + `Shift` + `W`

Increase point size .... `Ctrl` + `Shift` + `>`

Format—Paragraph

*Enhances text and changes appearances of para-
graphs and entire documents. You can emphasize
special paragraphs by setting tabs, changing the
alignment, indenting, controlling page breaks, and
so on. The following table displays the paragraph
formatting options available. For more information
on each of the options, see "Page Breaks," "Formatting—Toolbar," "Format—Character,"
"Styles—Create," or "Standard Toolbar."*

Collect and store paragraph formats to
create a style guide for a document. For
more information, see "Style—Create."

Option	Description
Alignment	
Left	Hugs the left margin.
Right	Hugs the right margin.
Centered	Aligns equally between the right and left margins.
Justified	Spreads text between the left and right margins. (This choice is used more with newspaper columns because it makes every line the same length by changing the spacing between the letters to make it fit.)
Indentation	
Left	Indents the paragraph from the left margin.
Right	Indents the paragraph from the right margin.
Spacing	
Before	Defines the amount of spacing before a paragraph. Enter the amount of space in increments of 1/2 line.

After	Defines the amount of spacing after a paragraph. Enter the amount of space in increments of 1/2 line.
Line Spacing	Defines the line spacing automatically by the tallest character on each line. To change spacing, choose Single (1 line), 1 1/2 (1 1/2 lines), or Double (2 lines) between lines of text.
At	Defines a customized amount of space between the lines.

Pagination

Page Break Before	Inserts the page break before the specified paragraph, bumping the paragraph to the next page.
Keep With Next	Keeps the specified paragraph and the next paragraph together.
Keep Lines Together	Keeps all the lines of the paragraph together.

Widow\Orphan Control	Prevents the appearance of a single word on the last line.

Line Numbers

Suppress Line Numbers	Ignores the line numbers you may have chosen under "Lines—Number."
Don't Hyphenate	Prevents words from being hyphenated.

Mouse Steps

1. Select the text you want to format.

2. Click on the Format menu.

3. Click on the Paragraph command.

4. Click on the paragraph format options from the table above.

5. The effects you have assigned to the text will be displayed in the Preview box. Make sure you like the current specifications.

6. To apply paragraph formats, click OK.

Keyboard Steps

1. Highlight the paragraph you want to format, or highlight the whole document by pressing .... Ctrl + 5

(on the keypad)

2. Pull down the Format menu .... [Alt] + [O]

3. Choose **P**aragraph .... [P]

4. Choose from the paragraph format options in the preceding table .... [Alt] + *underlined letter*

5. The effects you have assigned to the text will be displayed in the Preview box. Make sure you like the current specifications.

6. To apply paragraph formats, press .... [↵]

Enhancement	**Key Combination**
Centers paragraph	[Ctrl] + [E]
Double-spaces paragraphs	[Ctrl] + [2]
Creates hanging indent	[Ctrl] + [T]
Indents from the left	[Ctrl] + [M]
Justifies paragraph	[Ctrl] + [J]
Left-aligns paragraph	[Ctrl] + [L]
Removes formatting	[Ctrl] + [Q]
Right-aligns paragraph	[Ctrl] + [R]
Single-spaces paragraph	[Ctrl] + [1]

Formatting Toolbar

Formats characters and paragraphs quickly. Use the mouse or keyboard to highlight text, and with the mouse click on one of the buttons from the

Formatting toolbar. Each button works as a toggle: click it to turn on the effect, and click it again to turn off the effect. See the inside back cover of this book for a listing of the tools on the Formatting toolbar.

Formatting Toolbar—Display

Displays the Formatting toolbar across the top of the window.

TIP

To hide the Formatting toolbar, repeat the same steps.

Mouse Steps

1. Click on the View menu.

2. Click on **Toolbars**.

3. Click on **Formatting** in the Toolbars list box.

4. Click on **OK**.

Keyboard Steps

1. Pull down the View menu .... `Alt` + `V`

2. Select **Toolbars** .... `T`

3. From the Toolbars list box,
   choose **Formatting** .... `↑` or `↓`

4. Choose **OK** .... `⏎`

Frame

Creates a frame (border) around a block of text, a graphic, or a chart.

Mouse Steps

1. Click on the **View** menu.

2. Click on the **Page** Layout command.

3. Select the text, the graphic, or the chart you want to enclose in a frame.

4. Click on the **Insert** menu.

5. Click on the **Frame** command.

Keyboard Steps

1. Pull down the **View** menu .... Alt + V

2. Choose **Page** Layout .... P

3. Select the text, the graphic, or the chart you want to enclose in a frame. (See "Select—Text.")

4. Pull down the **Insert** menu .... Alt + I

5. Choose **Frame** .... F

TIP

To delete a frame, select it by dragging the I-beam pointer to highlight the contents of a frame. Open the **Edit** menu and choose Undo Insert Frame. To delete the frame and the objects inside of it, press **Delete**.

Grammar Checker

*Checks the grammar within the document. How-
ever, it does not eliminate the need for checking the
grammar yourself. It also explains grammatical
rules and allows you to ignore or change them.*

TIP

If you forgot to start at the beginning,
when the grammar checker finishes at the
end of the file, Word will ask you, "Do you
want to continue checking at the begining
of the document?" You can answer this
question by choosing Yes (press **Y**), by
choosing No (press **N**), or by choosing
Help (press **H**). If you start at the begin
ning of the document instead of in the
middle, Word will not ask this question.

Mouse Steps

1. Go to the top of the document.

2. Click on the **Tools** menu.

3. Click on the **Grammar** command.

4. To correct an error that the Grammar Checker
    has found, select one of these options:

Option	Description
Ignore	Skips over the suggested correction, neglecting to make the correction.
Change	Makes the correction.

Next Sentence	Skips over the current suggestion and continues on the next sentence.
Ignore **R**ule	Ignores the rule in the **S**uggestions box throughout the rest of the document.
Close or Cancel	Stops Grammar Checker without checking through the end of the document.
Explain	Gives information about the grammatical rule.
Options	Allows you to change the rule.
Undo **L**ast	Returns to the last change.

5. After you read the contents of the Readability Statistics box, click **OK**.

Keyboard Steps

1. Go to the top of the document, by pressing .... Ctrl + Alt

2. Pull down the Tools menu .... Alt + T

3. Choose **G**rammar .... G

4. To correct an error that the Grammar Checker has found, select one of these options:

Option	Description	Press...
Ignore	Skips over the correction it suggests, neglecting to make the correction.	Alt + I
Change	Makes the correction.	Alt + C
Next Sentence	Skips over the current suggestion and continues on the next sentence.	Alt + N
Ignore Rule	Ignores the rule in the Suggestions box throughout the rest of the document.	Alt + R
Close or Cancel	Stops Grammar Checker without checking through the end of the document.	Esc
Explain	Gives information about the grammatical rule.	Alt + E
Options	Allows you to change the rule.	Alt + O

Undo **Last** Returns to the last
change.

5. After you read the contents of the
Readability Statistics box, press ....⏎

 If Word finds a spelling error, it will
automatically open the Spelling dialog box
on top of the Grammar dialog box. For
TIP more information about the Spelling
option, see "Spell Check."

Graphic—Import

*Creates an invisible graphics frame into which it
places graphics that you import from another
program. To delete the graphic, you have to delete
the graphic frame. For more information on deleting the graphic frame, see "Graphics—Frame."*

 If you plan to import and export documents and graphics, select the Complete
installation option when you install Word
TIP for Windows 6.0. Check your documentation for more information.

Mouse Steps

1. Click on the **View** menu.

2. Click on the **P**age Layout command.

 Press the **Page Layout View** button at the
bottom left corner of the screen as an
TIP alternative to steps 1 and 2.

3. Position the cursor where you want to insert the graphic.

4. Click on the **Insert** menu.

5. Click on the **Picture** command to open the Insert Picture dialog box.

6. Click on a graphic file to import in the File Name list box.

7. To view the graphic, make sure the **Preview** Picture check box is turned on.

8. To insert the graphic in the document at the cursor, click **OK**.

Keyboard Steps

1. Pull down the View menu ....`Alt` + `V`

2. Choose **Page** Layout ....`P`

3. Position the cursor where you want to insert the graphic ....`↑` `↓` `←` `→`

4. Pull down the Insert menu ....`Alt` + `I`

5. Choose **Picture** to open the Insert Picture dialog box ....`P`

6. Activate the File **Name** list box ....`Alt` + `N`

                                   `Tab`

7. Choose the graphic file to import .....`↑` or `↓`

TIP

To import a picture, look for the file extensions .BMP or .PCX. If you want to import a piece of clip art, go to the \winword6\clipart subdirectory and look for files with the file extension .WMF.

8. To view the graphic, make sure the **P**review Picture check box is turned on ....[Alt] + [P]

9. To insert the graphic in the document at the cursor, press...[↵]

Graphics—Frame

Creates a frame in which you can place a graphic or type text. See also "Object—Embed," "Objects Embedded—Delete," or "Objects Embedded—Update."

Mouse Steps

TIP

To add a frame quickly, click on the **Insert Frame** button on either the Drawing toolbar or the Forms toolbar.

1. Click on the **V**iew menu.

2. Click on the **P**age Layout command.

3. Highlight the text where you want to insert the frame.

4. Click on the **I**nsert menu.

5. Click on the **F**rame command.

To delete a graphics frame or a graphic, click anywhere in the graphics frame and press **Delete**.

TIP

Keyboard Steps

1. Pull down the View menu .... $\boxed{\text{Alt}}$ + $\boxed{\text{V}}$

2. Choose Page Layout .... $\boxed{\text{P}}$

3. Highlight the section of text where you want to insert the frame .... $\boxed{\text{Ctrl}}$ + $\boxed{\text{Shift}}$ + $\boxed{\downarrow}$

4. Pull down the Insert menu .... $\boxed{\text{Alt}}$ + $\boxed{\text{I}}$

5. Choose Frame .... $\boxed{\text{F}}$

The mouse pointer has a four-headed arrow attached to it when it's in the frame.

TIP

Headers and Footers

Inserts predetermined information, such as chapter titles, dates, or page numbers, along the top or bottom margin of every printed page (or every other printed page) as you print your document.

Mouse Steps

1. Click on the View menu.

2. Click on the Header and Footer command.

3. **(Optional)** If you want a footer, click on the **Switch Between Header and Footer** button on the Header and Footer toolbar. (It's the button on the far left.)

4. Type the text for the header or footer in the area surrounded by a dashed line.

5. To insert the current page number in the header or footer, click on the **Page number** button. To insert the current date in the header or footer, click on the **Date** button. To insert the current time in the header or footer, click on the **Time** button.

6. Click on **Close** when you are finished.

7. View header and footer information on-screen either by clicking the View menu and choosing the **Page** Layout command, or by clicking the **File** menu and choosing the Print Preview command.

Keyboard Steps

1. Pull down the View menu .... Alt + V

2. Choose Header and Footer .... H

3. **(Optional)** If you want a footer, click the **Switch Between Header and Footer** button

on the Header and Footer toolbar. (It's the
button on the far left.)

4. Type the text for the header or
footer in the area surrounded by a
dashed line ....*text*

EXAMPLE An example of useful header or footer
information is the title of a chapter,
assignment number, date, page number,
time, and author.

5. Use the following list for shortcuts
to enter the current page number,
date, and time:

Description	Press...
To insert the current page number in the header or footer	Alt + Shift + P
To insert the current date in the header or footer	Alt + Shift + D
To insert the current time in the header or footer	Alt + Shift + T

6. Close the header/footer
area and return to the
document when you
are finished ....Alt + Shift + C

7. View header and footer information
on-screen either by pulling down

the View menu and choosing the
Page Layout command or by pulling
down the **File** menu and choosing
the Print Preview command ..... Alt + V , P
or Alt + F , V

Help

*Provides on-screen, step-by-step instructions at any
time you are working on a document and need
help. It also provides instructions to help you learn
basic or advanced features.*

Mouse Steps

1. Click on the **Help** menu.

2. Select the Contents command.

3. Select one of the following topics to move
    around the Help window quickly:

Button	Description
Contents	Provides a list of topics to choose from.
Search	Finds a topic quickly without using arrow keys, PgUp, or PgDn.
Back	Moves back to the preceding topic.
History	Displays a list of the last help topics you viewed up to 40.

| Index | Displays an alphabetical listing of topics. |

4. **(Optional)** To print the topic information, click on the Help window's **File** menu.

5. **(Optional)** Click on the **Print** Topic command.

6. Return to the document by double-clicking the Help window's Control-menu box (located in the upper left corner).

If you choose the History button, use the arrow keys to choose a topic that you want to view out of the 40 topics available. Press **Enter** to select a topic.

Keyboard Steps

1. Pull down the **Help** menu .... `Alt` + `H`

2. Choose **Contents** .... `C`

3. To locate a specific topic, select **Search** ....`Alt` + `S`

4. Enter the topic name ....*text*

5. Press ....`⏎`

6. Scroll through the list of possible topics ....`↑` or `↓`

7. Choose **Go** To ....`Alt` + `G`

8. The topic will appear in a How To box. Scroll through the information ....`↑` or `↓`

9. **(Optional)** To print the topic
   information, click on the Help
   window's File menu .... Alt + F

10. **(Optional)** Select the Print
    Topic command .... P

11. To return to the document,
    select the File menu .... Alt + F

12. Choose Exit X

Use the following table to move around the Help
window quickly.

Button	Press...	Description
Contents	Alt + C	Provides a list of topics to choose from.
Search	Alt + S	After you've typed the topic in the Search dialog box, Word finds a topic quickly without your using arrow keys, PgUp, or PgDn.
Back	Alt + B	Moves back to the preceding topic.
History	Alt + T	Displays a list of the last help topics you have viewed up to 40.

Index   **Alt** + **I**   Displays an
alphabetical listing
of topics.

Hyphenate

Reduces the ragged appearance of unjustified text and allows you to fit more text on a page.

Mouse Steps

1. Open the **Tools** menu.

2. Choose **Hyphenation**.

3. Select the **Automatically Hyphenate Document** check box.

4. In the Hyphenation **Zone** box, type or select the amount of space between the last word in the line and the right margin.

TIP

To reduce the number of hyphens, make the hyphenation zone wider. To reduce raggedness, make it narrower.

5. In the **Limit Consecutive Hyphens To** box, select the number of lines that can be hyphenated.

6. Choose **OK**.

Keyboard Steps

1. Select the Tools menu .... `Alt` + `T`

2. Choose Hyphenation .... `H`

3. Select the Automatically Hyphenate
   Document check box .... `Alt` + `A`

4. In the Hyphenation Zone box,
   type or select the amount of
   space between last word in line
   and right margin .... `Alt` + `Z`
   `↑` or `↓`

5. In the Limit Consecutive Hyphens
   To box, select the number of
   lines that can be hyphenated .... `Alt` + `L`
   `↑` or `↓`

6. Press .... `↵`

Indent—Insert

Changes the alignment of text by either moving it closer to the left margin or closer to the right margin.

Mouse Steps

TIP

Quickly indent or unindent highlighted text by clicking on the **Indent** or **Unindent** buttons on the Formatting toolbar. Clicking on either option moves the text .5 inch.

1. Position the cursor in the paragraph you want to indent. If you want to indent more than one paragraph, highlight them.

2. Click on the Format menu.

3. Click on the Paragraph command.

4. Click on an option from the Indentation options:

Left	Enter a positive or negative number to specify the placement of the entire paragraph in regards to the right or left of the left margin.
Right	Enter a positive or negative number to specify the placement of the entire paragraph in regards to the right or left of the right margin.
Special	Select to indent first line of paragraph or to create a hanging indent.

5. To activate the indent option, click OK.

Keyboard Steps

1. Position the cursor in the paragraph you want to indent. If you want to indent more than one paragraph, highlight them.

2. Pull down the Format menu .... Alt + O

3. Choose Paragraph .... P

4. Choose an option from the Indentation options:

Left .... Alt + L
Then enter a positive or negative
number to specify the placement of
the entire paragraph in regards to the
right or left of the left margin .... #
↑ ↓

Right .... Alt + R
Then enter a positive or negative
number to specify the placement of
the entire paragraph in regards to
the right or left of the right margin .... #
↑ ↓

Special .... Alt + S
Indicate whether to indent the first
line or create a hanging indent .... ↑ ↓

5. To activate the indent option, press .... ⏎

Index—Compile

Sorts all entries and arranges them into alphabeti-cal order.

Mouse Steps

1. Position the cursor where you want to begin indexing.

2. From the Insert menu, choose Index and Tables.

3. Select the Index tab.

4. In the Formats box, select the index format you want.

5. Choose one or more of the following:

To	Select this
Align page numbers with right margin	Right Align Page Numbers check box.
Format index with multiple columns	In the Columns box, type or select a number.
Insert tab leader characters	In the Tab Leader box, select the leader you want.

6. Choose **OK**.

EXAMPLE

Some indexes are separated by alphabetized letters. Under the A header are all the entries that start with A.

TIP

To update or display an index, position the insertion point in the index and click the right mouse button or press **Shift+F10**. Then choose **Update Field** from the QuickMenu.

Keyboard Steps

1. Position the cursor where you want to begin indexing.

2. From the Insert menu, choose Index and Tables .... Alt + I
   X

3. Select the Index tab .... Alt + X

4. In the Format box, select the index format you want .... Alt + T

5. Choose one or more of the following:

To	Select this
Align page numbers with right margin	**Right** Align Page Numbers check box.
Format index with multiple columns	In the **Columns** box, type or select a number.
Insert tab leader characters	In the **Tab** Leader box, select the leader you want.

6. Choose OK .... ⏎

Index—Create Entry

Creates an index based on main entries, subentries, and cross-references. The index entries appear in an alphabetized list that's usually placed at the end of the document.

Mouse Steps

1. Highlight the text that you want to mark as an index entry.

2. Click on the Insert menu.

3. Click on Index and Tables.

4. Select Mark Entry.

5. **(Optional)** Choose one or more of the following options:

Main Entry	Allows you to edit the selected text.
Subentry	Creates a secondary entry under the main entry.
Cross-reference	Creates a cross-reference (*See* or *See also*) for an index entry.
Current Page or Page Range	Creates a page range for the entry.

6. Select one of the following:

Mark	To mark the index entry.
Mark All	To mark all the occurrences of the same text.

7. Click on **Close**.

Keyboard Steps

1. Highlight the text that you want to mark as an index entry .... **Ctrl** + **Shift** + **↑** **↓** **←** **→**

2. Choose the Insert menu .... **Alt** + **I**

3. Select Index and Tables .... **X**

4. Select Mark Entry .... **Alt** + **K**

5. **(Optional)** Choose one or more of the following options:

Main Entry	Allows you to edit the selected text **Alt** + **E**
Subentry	Creates a secondary entry under the main entry **Alt** + **S**
Cross-reference	Creates a cross-reference (*See* or *See also*) for an index entry **Alt** + **C**
Current **Page** or **Page Range**	Creates a page range for the entry **Alt** + **P** or **Alt** + **R**

6. Select one of the following:

Mark	To mark the index entry **Alt** + **M**

Mark **All**   To mark all the
                        occurrences of the
                        same text   Alt + A

7. Press .... ↵

Index—Entry Update

*Generates an updated index after you make
document or format changes.*

Mouse Steps

1. Select the Insert menu.

2. Choose Index and Tables.

3. Select the Index tab and then choose **OK**.

4. Word will ask if you want to replace the
   existing index. Choose **Yes**.

> You can quickly update an index by
> placing the insertion point in the INDEX
> field and pressing **F9**.

TIP

Keyboard Steps

1. Select the Insert menu .... Alt + I

2. Choose Index and Tables........................... X

3. Select the Index tab and then
   choose OK .... Alt + X

4. Word will ask if you want to replace the
   existing index. Choose Yes ....

Labels—Create

*Use a mailing label template to create a label
format, attach a data file, and create a label layout. Creates labels that you can mail. Prints a text
label on plain paper when you choose the Only
Check for Error button from the Print Merge
toolbar.*

To print sets of mailing labels by opening
the main document, pull down the **File**
menu (press **Alt+F**) and choose the Print
Merge command (press **M**).

TIP

Mouse Steps

1. Pull down the Tools menu.

2. Choose Envelopes and Labels.

3. Click on the Labels tab.

4. Type the address.

5. **(Optional)** To change the return address,
   select Use **Return** Address and enter the
   return address.

6. **(Optional)** To print only a single label,
   choose Single Label. To print a full page
   of the same label, choose Full Page of the
   Same Label.

7. Select **Print**.

Keyboard Steps

1. Pull down the Tools menu .... `Alt` + `T`

2. Choose Envelopes and Labels .... `E`

3. Choose the Labels tab .... `Alt` + `A`

4. Enter the address .... *text*

5. **(Optional)** To create the return
   address, select Use Return
   Address .... `Alt` + `R`
   Enter the return address .... *text*

6. **(Optional)** To print only a single
   label, choose Single Label .... `Alt` + `N`
   To print a full page of the same
   label, choose Full Page of the
   Same Label .... `Alt` + `F`

7. Select Print .... `Alt` + `P`

Line Spacing—Adjust

Improves the appearance of the document by adjusting the line spacing and the line height. You can choose from the following:

Option	Description
Single	Single spacing, no additional space between lines.
1.5 Lines	1 1/2 spacing, adds an additional 1/2 line of space between lines of text.

Double	Double spacing, adds one additional line of space between lines of text.
At Least	Specifies a minimum amount of space between lines.
Exactly	Specifies a fixed amount of space.
Multiple	Triple spacing, adds two additional lines of space between the lines.
At	If you selected At Least, Exactly, or Multiple, use this option to define a customized amount of space between the lines.

Mouse Steps

1. Select the text for which you want to adjust the line spacing.

2. Click on the Format menu.

3. Click on the **P**aragraph command.

4. Click on the **Li**ne spacing drop-down box and choose one of the options from the preceding table under "Line Spacing."

5. To adjust the spacing with the current options, click **OK**.

Keyboard Steps

1. Select the text for which you want to adjust the line spacing.

2. Pull down the Format menu .... `Alt` + `O`

3. Choose **P**aragraph .... `P`

4. Activate the Li**n**e spacing drop-down box .... `Alt` + `N`

   `↑` or `↓`

5. Choose one of the options from the preceding table under "Line Spacing" .... `↑` or `↓`

TIP For quick adjustment without leaving your document, use these shortcuts: press **Ctrl+1** for single spacing; press **Ctrl+5** for 1 1/2; press **Ctrl+2** for double spacing.

6. To adjust the spacing with the current options, press .... `←`

Link

Forms a link between a different application and Word for Windows 6.0.

Mouse Steps

1. Start the other application and open the file that contains the information you want to link to a Word document.

2. Highlight the information you want to link.

3. Click on the **Edit** menu.

4. To copy information to the Clipboard, click on the **Copy** command.

5. Start Word for Windows.

6. Open your Word document (see "Open— Document/File") and position the cursor where you want to establish the link.

7. Click on the **Edit** menu.

8. Click on the Paste **Special** command.

9. Click on the Paste **Link** button.

10. If you want to use a format other than the one highlighted in the **As** list box, click on a different format.

11. Click on **OK**.

Keyboard Steps

1. Start the other application and open the file that contains the information you want to link to a Word document.

2. Highlight the information you want to link.

3. Pull down the **Edit** menu ....`Alt` + `E`

4. To copy information to the Clipboard, choose Copy ....`C`

5. Start Word for Windows.

6. Open your Word document (see "Open—Document/File") and position the cursor where you want to establish the link.

7. Pull down the Edit menu ....`Alt` + `E`

8. Choose Paste Special ....`S`

9. Choose Paste Link ....`Alt` + `L`

10. If you want to use a format other than the one highlighted in the As list box, choose a different format ....`Alt` + `A`

    `↑` or `↓`

11. Choose **OK** ....`⏎`

Links—Update

When you change the information in an original document in another application, Word will automatically update that document in the Word for Windows application. You can change the way the links are updated, though. To do so, follow these steps.

Mouse Steps

1. Click on the Edit menu.

2. Click on the Links command.

3. Depending on how you want to update your

documents, click on one of the following
options from the Update options box:

Automatic	Updates linked file automatically as original file is updated.
Manual	Updates linked file when you choose to update it. When you want to update a linked file, click the Update Now button.
Update Now button	Updates linked files immediately when you press it.

Keyboard Steps

1. Pull down the Edit menu .... `Alt` + `E`

2. Choose Links .... `K`

3. Depending on how you want to update your documents, choose one of the following options from the Update options box:

Option	Description	Press...
Automatic	Updates linked file automatically as original file is updated	`Alt` + `A`
Manual	Updates linked file when you choose to update it	`Alt` + `M`

| Update Now button | Updates linked files immediately when you press it | Alt + U |

Lists

See "Bullet—Add," "Bullet—Delete," or "Numbered List— Create."

Macro—Assign to a Menu or Toolbar

Assigns a series of actions to a menu or toolbar button. This can only be accomplished with a mouse.

Mouse Steps

1. With the toolbar displayed, click on the **Tools** menu.

2. Click on **Customize.**

3. Choose the **T**oolbars tab.

4. In the Save Changes In box, select the template in which the macro is stored.

5. In Categories box, select **Macros**.

6. From the Macros list box, drag the macro name to the toolbar on the desktop to which you want to add it. A button outline will be visible.

TIP

Since macros don't have built-in buttons, a blank button appears on the toolbar and the custom button dialog box appears.

7. In the Button box, select one of the following:

   To place an image on the blank button, select the image.

   To create a button with text on it, first click the button, and then type the text at the bottom of the dialog box.

8. Choose Assign button and select **Close**.

Macro—Record

Records a series of actions or keystrokes so that you can quickly repeat them in any of your documents.

Mouse Steps

1. Click on the Tools menu.

2. Select Macro.

3. Click on the Record button.

4. In the Record Macro Name text box, type a name for the macro or use the default name assigned.

5. To type a small description of the macro, click on the Description text box.

6. To record the macro, click **OK**.

TIP

REC on the status bar means Word is recording every keystroke you make.

7. Choose the commands you want to include in the macro with the keyboard. Word will not accept any commands using the mouse.

8. When you are finished adding commands to include in the macro, click on the **Stop** button on the Macro Record toolbar.

Keyboard Steps

1. Pull down the Tools menu .... Alt + T

2. Select Macro .... M

3. Choose the Record button .... Alt + O

4. In the Record Macro Name text box, type a name for the macro or use the default name assigned .... *text*

5. To type a small description of the macro, activate the Description text box .... Alt + D

6. To record the macro, press .... ⏎

7. Choose the commands you want to include in the macro. Remember that these commands will only be

accepted if performed on the keyboard; Word does not accept mouse steps while recording.

8. When you are finished adding commands to include in the macro, pull down the Tools menu and select **Macro** ....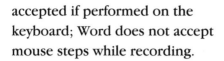

9. Choose Stop Recording ....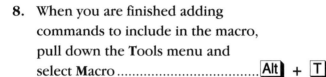

10. Choose Close ....

Macro—Run

Activates the series of commands you recorded, repeating the keystrokes or actions.

Mouse Steps

1. Click on the Tools menu.

2. Click on the Macro command.

3. Click on the macro you want to run from the Macro Name list.

4. Click on the Run button.

Keyboard Steps

1. Pull down the Tools menu ....

2. Choose **M**acro .... M

3. Choose the macro you want to run
   from the **M**acro Name list .... Alt + M

   ↑ or ↓

4. Choose **R**un .... Alt + R

Mail Merge—Create Main Document

Creating a mail merge is a three-step process that involves creating the main document (described here), creating a data source (see "Data Source—Create"), and then merging the two together (see "Mail Merge—Merge with Data Source").

Mouse Steps

1. Pull down the Tools menu.

2. Select Mail Merge.

3. Under Main document, choose the Create button.

4. Select Form Letters.

5. Choose the Active Window button.

6. Under the Create button, Word displays the type of merge it will perform and the name of the main document.

7. Press **Close**.

Keyboard Steps

1. Pull down the Tools menu .... `Alt` + `T`

2. Select Mail Merge .... `R`

3. Under Main document, choose the
   Create button .... `Alt` + `C`

4. Select Form Letters .... `L`

5. Choose the Active Window button .... `A`

6. Under the Create button, Word
   displays the type of merge it will
   perform and the name of the main
   document.

7. Press .... `Tab`

   `⏎`

TIP

When you begin setting up a merge, the
Print Merge toolbar appears below the
other toolbars that are visible at the top of
the screen.

Mail Merge—Merge with Data Source

*Once you have completed the first two steps, setting
up a main document (such as a form letter) and
creating a data source, you are ready for the final
step—creating a merged form letter.*

Mouse Steps

1. Click on the Tools menu.

2. Click on Mail Merge.

3. Choose the **Merge** button.

4. **(Optional)** You can merge the information to a New Document or to the Printer.

5. Select **Merge**.

To view additional records, click one of the **Go To Record** arrow buttons on the Mail Merge toolbar. To print the form letters, click on the **Print** button on the Mail Merge toolbar.

Click the **View Merged Data** button on the Mail Merge toolbar to view the merged documents before printing.

Keyboard Steps

1. Pull down the Tools menu .... `Alt` + `T`

2. Select Mail Merge .... `R`

3. Choose the Merge button .... `Alt` + `M`

4. **(Optional)** You can merge the information with a New Document or the Printer .... `Alt` + `R`

   `↑` or `↓`

5. Select Merge ....`Alt` + `M`

Margins—Page Setup Command

Use the Page Setup command to set the margin. Adjust the way the document appears on the paper, including proximity to the left, right, top, and bottom edges of the paper. See also "Ruler."

TIP

The default setting for the left and right margins is 1.25 inches.

Mouse Steps

1. Position the cursor where you want to change the margins, or highlight the text for which you want to adjust the margins.

2. Click on the **File** menu.

3. Click on the Page Set**up** command.

4. Click on the **Margins** tab.

5. Click on the text boxes that contain the margins you want to change: **T**op, **B**ottom, **L**eft, or **R**ight.

6. Type in the new measurement.

7. To set new margins, click **OK**.

TIP

To display the new margins setup, click on the View menu, and then click on the Page Layout command.

Keyboard Steps

1. Position the cursor where you want to change the margins, or highlight text for which you want to adjust the margins.

2. Pull down the File menu ....| Alt | + | F |

3. Choose Page Setup ....| U |

4. Choose Margins ....| M |

5. Activate the text boxes for the margins you want to change:

   Top ....| Alt | + | T |

   Bottom ....| Alt | + | B |

   Left ....| Alt | + | F |

   Right ....| Alt | + | G |

6. Enter the new measurement ....###

7. To set new margins, press ....| ⏎ |

TIP
To display the new margins setup, pull down the View menu (press **Alt+V**) and choose **P**age Layout (press **P**).

Merge—Add Information to Data Source

See "Data Source—Adding Information."

Merge—Create Data Source

See "Data Source—Create."

Merge—Create Main Document File

See "Mail Merge—Create Main Document."

New Document—Create

Creates a new document. See also "AutoText Entry—Create," "Forms—Create," "Labels—Create," "Mail Merge—Create Main Document," "Numbered List—Create," "Style—Create," "Table—Create," or "Template—Create."

Mouse Steps

1. Open the File menu.

2. Choose New.

3. To base the document on a template, type the template name in the Template box or select it from the list. If you do not select a template, Word uses the Normal template.

4. Choose OK.

TIP

You can create a document quickly by clicking the **New** button on the Standard toolbar.

Keyboard Steps

1. Select the File menu ....[Alt] + [F]

2. Choose New ....[N]

3. To select a specific template, type its name in or choose it from the Template box ....[↑] or [↓]

4. Choose **OK** ....[↵]

Numbered List—Create

Formats selected text into a numbered list.

EXAMPLE

A good time to create a numbered list is when you are writing consecutive steps that the reader will have to follow. For instance, this book uses many numbered lists.

Mouse Steps

1. Highlight the text you want to change to a numbered list.

Quickly add numbers to a list by pressing the **Number List** button on the Formatting toolbar and skip steps 2 and 3.

TIP

2. Click on the Format menu.

3. Click on the Bullets and Numbering command.

To remove the numbered list formatting, click on the **Number List** button on the Formatting toolbar and the text will be restored to its original state.

TIP

4. Click on the Numbered List tab.

5. Click on the style of numbered list you want.

6. To create the numbered list, click **OK**.

Keyboard Steps

1. Highlight the text you want to change to a numbered list.

2. Pull down the Format menu .... `Alt` + `O`

3. Choose Bullets and Numbering .... `N`

4. Choose the Numbered tab .... `Alt` + `N`

5. Scroll through the styles and make your selection .... `↑` `↓` `←` or `→`

6. To create the numbered list, press .... `↵`

Object—Embed

An embedded object is an object that is created with an application other than the main application you are using. (In this case the main application would be Word for Windows 6.0.) By embedding the object in Word, you command the secondary application to send all the information it needs to produce the object in a foreign application. You can embed objects, charts, graphs, and pictures.

Some applications that embed objects easily into Word are Microsoft Excel, Draw, Graph, and the Equation Editor. To find other applications that embed objects easily, check your documentation.

TIP

Mouse Steps

1. Open the document and position the cursor where you want to embed the object. (See "Open—Document/File.")

2. Click on the **Insert** menu.

3. Click on the **Object** command.

4. To open the application in which you want to create the object, click on the application from the **Object** Type dialog box.

If the format is not on the list, the source application does not support embedded objects.

TIP

5. Create your object.

6. Click on the File menu.

7. To embed the object in your document, choose an Exit and Return to Document option. (Depending on the application, the actual command varies in wording.)

8. If you are asked if you want to Update *the object* in your document, click Yes.

Keyboard Steps

1. Open the document and position the cursor where you want to establish the link. (See "Open— Document/File.")

2. Pull down the Insert menu .... Alt + I

3. Choose Object .... O

4. To open the application in which you want to create the object, select the application from the Object Type dialog box .... ↑ or ↓

TIP

If the format is not on the list, the source application does not support embedded objects.

5. Create your object.

6. Pull down the File menu .... Alt + F

7. To embed the object in your document, choose an Exit and Return to Document option. (Depending on the application, the actual command varies in wording.) X

8. If you are asked if you want to Update *the object* in your document, press .... Y

Objects (Embedded)—Delete

Deletes the embedded object from your document. This can only be accomplished with a mouse.

Mouse Steps

1. Click on the object you want to delete.

2. Press **Ctrl+Shift+F9** to break the link.

3. Press **Delete**.

Objects (Embedded)—Update

Changes or updates an embedded object. Word opens a window in which you can edit objects.

Mouse Steps

1. To open the application in which the object was created, double-click on the object in the document.

2. Make the changes you want to the object.

3. Click on the File menu.

4. Choose Exit.

5. A dialog box will pop up asking whether you want to update the object. Click on **Yes**, **No**, or **Cancel**.

Keyboard Steps

1. Select the object you want to update.

2. Pull down the Edit menu .... `Alt` + `E`

3. Select Object .... `O`

4. Select Edit from the submenu .... `E`

5. Choose the application in which it was created .... `↑` or `↓`

    Press .... `⏎`

6. Make your changes to the object in the application.

7. Pull down the File menu .... `Alt` + `F`

8. Choose Exit .... `X`

TIP   The Exit choice varies depending upon which application you are working in. Some applications say Exit and Return to "document name" while others just say Exit.

9. A dialog box will pop up asking whether you want to update the object. Choose one of the following options and press **Enter**:

Yes .... $\boxed{Y}$

No .... $\boxed{N}$

Cancel .... $\boxed{Tab}$

$\boxed{\leftarrow}$

Open—Document/File

Opens the document you want to edit or update.

Mouse Steps

1. Click on the **File** menu.

2. Click on the **Open** command.

TIP

The shortcut for steps 1 and 2 is to click on the **Open** button on the Standard toolbar.

3. **(Optional)** If the document is on another drive, click on that drive in the **Drives** list box.
OR
If the document is in another directory, click on the directory in the **Directories** list box.

4. Double-click on the document name.

Keyboard Steps

1. Pull down the File menu .... Alt + F

2. Choose Open .... O

TIP

The shortcut for steps 1 and 2 is to press
Ctrl+O.

3. **(Optional)** If the document is on
   another drive, select the Drives
   list box and choose the correct
   drive .... Alt + V

   OR

   If the document is in another
   directory, select the **Directories** list
   box and choose the correct
   directory .... Alt + D
   ↑ ↓ ← →
   ↵

4. Return to the File Name text
   box and highlight the document
   name .... Alt + N

5. To open the document, press .... ↵

Outline—Create

Creates a structure by which you can outline the contents of a document. Word renumbers any elements that you move to another position. Word specifies if the headings have any subheadings underneath them by showing a plus (+) to the left of the heading. If there are no subheadings, Word displays a minus (–).

Mouse Steps

TIP

Move a heading by placing the mouse pointer over the + or –, dragging it to the new location, and dropping it.

1. Create a new document. (See "New Document—Create.")

2. Position the cursor where you want to begin the outline.

3. Click on the **View** menu.

4. Click on the **Outline** command.

5. Type text for the first header and press **Enter**.

   To insert another First-Level heading, type text and click on **Heading 1** from the drop-down list box.

   To insert a Subordinate Level heading, type text and click on the right arrow button.

To insert a Superior Level heading, type text and click on the left arrow button.

To insert Body Text, type text and click on the right double-headed arrow button.

Keyboard Steps

1. Open a new document. (See "New Document—Create.")

2. Position the cursor where you want to begin the outline.

3. Pull down the View menu .... `Alt` + `V`

4. Choose Outline .... `O`

5. Type text for the first header .... *text*

   Press .... `⏎`

   To insert another First-Level
   heading, type text .... *text*

   Press .... `⏎`

   To insert a Subordinate Level
   heading, type text .... *text*

   Press .... `Alt` + `Shift` + `→`

   `⏎`

   To insert a Superior Level heading,
   type text .... *text*

   Press .... `Alt` + `Shift` + `←`

   `⏎`

TIP

To continue creating subheads or body text, press **Alt+Shift+→**. To create higher level headers, reverse the process by pressing **Alt+Shift+←**.

Page—Number

Automatically applies a page number in the location you specify. Note that Word does not display page numbers in normal view. To view page numbers, choose Page Layout from the View menu.

Mouse Steps

1. Position the cursor on the page where you want numbering to begin.

2. Click on the Insert menu.

3. Click on the Page Numbers command.

4. Select the location from those listed under Position.

5. Select the alignment from the **Alignment** drop-down list box.

6. Begin numbering the pages by clicking **OK**.

Keyboard Steps

1. Position the cursor on the page where you want numbering to begin.

2. Pull down the Insert menu ....**Alt** + **I**

3. Choose Page Numbers ....**U**

4. Select the location from those
   listed under **P**osition .... Alt + P
   ↑ or ↓

5. Select alignment from the
   Alignment drop-down list box .... Alt + A
   ↑ or ↓

6. Begin numbering the pages
   by pressing .... ↵

Page Break (Hard)

*Specifies where one page ends and the next begins.
When you manually insert a page break it is called
a hard page break because it is not dependent upon
the amount of text filling up a whole page. Hard
page breaks appear as a single dotted line.*

Mouse Steps

1. Position the cursor where you want to insert a
   hard page break.

2. Click on the **I**nsert menu.

3. Click on the **B**reak command.

4. Click on the **P**age Break option.

5. Click **OK**.

Keyboard Steps

1. Position the cursor where you want to insert a
   hard page break.

2.   Press ....Ctrl + ⏎

TIP

To delete a hard page break, position the cursor below the line and press **Backspace**.

Page Breaks with Paragraphs

Once you decide which paragraphs can be broken over two pages and which ones need to be kept together, you can control where Word inserts the soft page breaks in your document.

Mouse Steps

1.   Highlight the paragraph you do not want broken by a soft page break.

2.   Click on the Format menu.

3.   Click on the Paragraph command.

4.   Select the Text Flow tab.

5.   From the Pagination options box, click on one of the following options:

Widow\Orphan Control	Prevents the appearance of a single line of the paragraph on one page.
Keep Lines Together	Keeps all the lines of the paragraph together.

Keep With Next	Keeps the specified paragraph and the next paragraph together.
Page Break Before	Inserts the page break before the selected paragraph, bumping the paragraph to the next page.

6. To return to the document, click **OK**.

Keyboard Steps

1. Highlight the paragraph you do not want broken by a soft page break.

2. Pull down the Format menu .... `Alt` + `O`

3. Choose **Paragraph** .... `P`

4. Select the Text Flow tab .... `Alt` + `F`

5. From the Pagination options box, choose one of the following options:

   Widow/Orphan Control prevents the appearance of a single line of the paragraph on one page .... `Alt` + `W`

   Keep Lines Together keeps all the lines of the paragraph together .... `Alt` + `K`

Keep With Next keeps the specified
paragraph and the next paragraph
together ....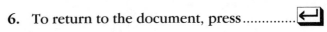

Page Break inserts the page break
before the selected paragraph
before bumping the paragraph to
the next page .... Alt + P

6. To return to the document, press.............. ⏎

TIP

To display the document with current
settings, pull down the View menu (press
Alt+V) and choose the **P**age Layout
command (press **P**), or pull down the File
menu (press **Alt+F**) and choose the Print
Preview command (press **V**).

Page Setup

*Page Setup refers to the size and orientation, mar-
gins, and paper source of the document with which
you are working. Sets page setup for the first time or
changes the old page setup to meet your current
needs. (The same steps apply regardless of whether
or not it's the first time.) In addition to custom
sizes, some of the sizes you have to choose from are
listed below.*

Size	Description
8 1/2" x 11"	Letter
8 1/2" x 14"	Legal

8.27" x 11.7"	A4 (European)
7.16" x 10.1"	B5

Mouse Steps

1. Position the cursor at the beginning of the document.

2. Click on the File menu.

3. Click on the Page Setup command.

4. Click on the Paper Size tab.

5. Click on a paper size from the Paper Size list box. Or you can specify a custom size by clicking on the Width and Height text boxes and typing in the custom size.

6. Choose a layout from the Orientation box:

Portrait	Is taller than it is wide and is the typical choice for letters and documents.
Landscape	Is wider than than it is tall and is better for spread-sheets, graphs, and some graphics.

7. The Preview box will show an example of the layout of your document. Check the Preview box to verify your choices.

8. Select how much of the document to apply the settings to with the **A**pply To drop-down list box.

9. To set (and finish changing) the paper size and orientation, click **OK**.

Keyboard Steps

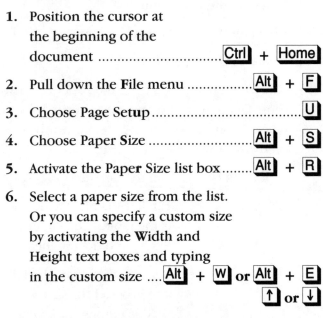

1. Position the cursor at the beginning of the document .... Ctrl + Home

2. Pull down the File menu .... Alt + F

3. Choose Page Setup .... U

4. Choose Paper Size .... Alt + S

5. Activate the Paper Size list box .... Alt + R

6. Select a paper size from the list. Or you can specify a custom size by activating the **W**idth and **H**eight text boxes and typing in the custom size .... Alt + W or Alt + E
↑ or ↓

7. Choose a layout from the Orientation box:

   Portrait is taller than it is wide and is the typical choice for letters and documents. To choose Portrait mode, press .... Alt + I

Landscape is wider than it is tall and is better for spreadsheets, graphs, and some graphics. To choose Landscape mode, press ....

8. The Preview box will show an example of the layout of your document. Check the Preview box to verify your choices.

9. To set the paper size and orientation, press ....

Paragraph

See "Format—Paragraph," "Indent—Insert," or "Line Spacing—Adjust."

Paste—Text

After copying or cutting text to the Clipboard, paste it into the same document, another document, or another Windows program.

Mouse Steps

1. Position the mouse pointer at the location you want the text inserted.

2. Click on the Edit menu.

3. Click on the Paste command.

Instead of using the **Edit Paste** command, you can use the **Paste** button located on the Standard toolbar to place text or graphics in the same document or other documents.

Keyboard Steps

1. Position the insertion point.

2. Select the **Edit** menu ....**Alt** + **E**

3. Select **Paste** ....**P**

Pressing **Ctrl+V** is a shortcut for steps 2 and 3.

Print—Document

Prints a document with your font and printer specifications.

Mouse Steps

To print a document using the shortcut, click on the **Print** button on the Standard toolbar.

1. To print the active document, click on the **File** menu.

2. Click on the **Print** command.

3. **(Optional)** Select your specifications from the following:

Click	Description
Print What	Prints the document, summary information and statistics, annotations, styles, key assignments, and AutoText entries.
Copies	Defines the number of copies to be printed.
Page Range	Defines the page numbers you want to print. Select from the following: **All**, Current Page, or Pages.
Print to File	Saves the printed document to another file.
Collate Copies	Prints one entire copy of the document before starting on the next copy.
Print	Prints all pages, or just even or odd pages.

4. To print the document with the current options, click on **OK**.

Keyboard Steps

1. To print the active document, pull down the File menu .... **Alt** + **F**

2. Choose **P**rint ....[P]

TIP

A shortcut for printing a document is to press **Ctrl+P**.

3. **(Optional)** Select your printer specifications from the following:

Option	Description	Press
Print What	Prints the document, summary information and statistics, annotations, styles, key assignments, and AutoText entries.	[Alt] + [P]
Copies	Defines the number of copies to be printed.	[Alt] + [C]
Page Range	Defines the page numbers to be printed (for example, to print pages 4–9, the range would be 4–9).	
	All	[Alt] + [A]
	Current Page	[Alt] + [E]
	Pages	[Alt] + [G]
Print to File	Saves the printed document to another file.	[Alt] + [L]

Collate Copies	Prints one entire copy of a document before starting the next copy.	Alt + I
Print	Prints all pages or just odd or even pages.	Alt + R

4. To print a document with the current options, press .... ↵

Printer Settings—Change

Allows you to choose a printer, change printer settings, and choose a paper source.

Mouse Steps

1. Click on the File menu.

2. Click on the Print command.

3. Select Printer to choose the printer.

4. Click on the Set as Default Printer button.

5. Click on Close.

6. (Optional) Click on the Options button and change the current settings on the Print tab. Click OK when you are finished.

7. To accept the current settings for the printer selection and setup and print the document, click on OK.

OR

To accept the current settings for the printer
and return to the document without printing,
click on **Close**.

Keyboard Steps

1. Pull down the File menu .... `Alt` + `F`

2. Choose **Print** .... `P`

3. Select Printer to choose the printer
    you want to use .... `↑` or `↓`
    `↵`

4. Choose Options .... `Alt` + `O`

5. Choose and change the current
    settings from the Print tab and press .... `↵`

6. To accept the current settings for the
    printer selection and setup and print
    the document, press .... `↵`
    OR
    To close the dialog box without
    printing, press .... `Esc`

Repeat

*Use this feature to repeat the preceding action,
command, or text you typed. This feature will not
repeat a series of actions, commands, or text typed,
only the latest one.*

Mouse Steps

1. Click on the **Edit** menu.

2. Click on the **Repeat** command.

TIP

If you change your mind or make a mistake, you can usually reverse the last several changes you made. Click on the **Undo** button to reverse the last action or the **Redo** button to redo the last canceled action. Both are located on the Standard toolbar.

Keyboard Steps

1. Pull down the Edit menu .... **Alt** + **E**

2. Choose **Repeat** .... **R**

TIP

Use the shortcut, **F4**, to repeat an action.

Revision Marks—Accept or Reject

After a document has been edited with revision marks, you can review the marks in the document and accept, reject, or ignore each change.

Mouse Steps

1. Click on the **Tools** menu.

2. Click on Revisions.

3. Choose the **R**eview button.

4. To move to a revision mark, click the appropriate Find button to search through the document.

5. Select one or more of the following:

Press	To
Accept	Accept a revision.
Reject	Reject a revision.
Find ← or Find →	Leave the revision mark unchanged and move to next revision.
Undo Last	Undo the last acceptance or rejection.

6. Choose **Close**.

TIP

To quickly move to the next revision mark while reviewing the revisions, select the Find Next After Accept/Reject check box.

Keyboard Steps

1. Select Tools menu ....Alt + T

2. Choose Revisions V

3. Choose the **R**eview button ....Alt + R

4. To move to a revision mark, click the appropriate Find

button to search through the
document .... Alt + I

or

Alt + F

5. Select one or more of the following:

To	Description	Press
Accept	Accept a revision	Alt + A
Reject	Reject a revision	Alt + R
Find ← or Find →	Leave the revision mark unchanged and move to next revision	Alt + I or Alt + F
Undo Last	Undo the last acceptance or rejection	Alt + U

6. Choose **Close** .... Esc

Revision Marks—Display

*Displays revision bars in the margins, specialized
formatted characters to indicate inserted text, and
strikethru characters to indicate deleted text.*

Mouse Steps

1. Open the document you want to revise (see
   "Open—Document/File").

2. Click on the **To**ols menu.

3. Click on the Revisions command.

4. Click on the Mark Revisions While Editing check box.

TIP

To hide revision marks, deselect the Mark Revisions While Editing check box by clicking on it until the check mark is deleted. To return to the document, click **OK**.

5. Click on one or both of the following options for revision bars:

   Show Revisions on Screen

   Show Revisions in Printed Document

6. **(Optional)** Select Options to click on a format for the inserted, deleted, or revised text. Click **OK** when you are finished.

7. To save your choices and return to the document, click **OK**.

Keyboard Steps

1. Open the document you want to revise (see "Open—Document/File").

2. Pull down the Tools menu .... **Alt** + **T**

3. Choose Revisions .... **V**

4. Check the Mark Revisions While Editing check box .... **Alt** + **M**

TIP

To hide revision marks, deselect the **Mark** Revisions While Editing check box (press **Alt+M**). To return to the document, press **Enter**.

5. Choose one or both of the following options for revision bars:

Show Revisions on Screen ....**Alt** + **S**

Show Revisions in Printed Document ....**Alt** + **P**

6. **(Optional)** Select Options to choose a format for the inserted, deleted, or revised text....................**Alt** + **O** **←**

7. To save your choices and return to the document, press ....**←**

Revision Marks—Use

Displays specific character formatting in the text to indicate inserted and deleted text.

Mouse Steps

TIP

In order to see the revisions as you edit, select the **Mark** Revisions While Editing check box from the Revisions dialog box.

1. Open the document you want to revise (see "Open—Document/File").

2. Add text to the document. The text you add
   should have the character format you specified
   in the Revisions dialog box.

3. To delete text, highlight it.

4. Press **Delete**.

TIP

If you haven't changed the default in the
Revision Marks dialog box, added text is
underlined, and deleted text is formatted
as strikethru.

Keyboard Steps

1. Open the document you want
   to revise (see "Open—
   Document/File").

2. Add text to the document. The
   text you add should have the
   character format you specified in
   the Revisions Options dialog box...............*text*

3. To delete text, highlight it.

4. Press ....⌨Delete

Ruler

*Use the mouse to activate these commands on the
Ruler. (See also "Ruler—Display," "Columns—
Newspaper," "Format—Paragraphs,"
"Margins—Page Setup Command," "Formatting
Toolbar," "Table—Create," and "Tab—Change.")*

To set tabs	Highlight the text and click the Tab Alignment button at the far left of the horizontal ruler until you have selected the tab alignment you want (left, center, right or decimal). On the Ruler, click where you want to set a tab stop.
To set left and right margins	To set new margins, click on the markers (gray triangles) located on the left and right side of the Ruler and drag them to their new locations.
To indent paragraphs	Highlight paragraphs and click on the bottom indent marker (a gray triangle) on the left side of the Ruler and drag it to its new location.
To adjust column width	Make sure columns are formatted already. Select the text or position the insertion point in the indented paragraph, and drag the column marker where you want it.

Ruler—Display

Displays the Ruler across the top of the window.

Mouse Steps

1. Click on the View menu.

2. To display the Ruler, click on the **Ruler** command.

To hide the Ruler, repeat the same steps.

Keyboard Steps

1. Pull down the View menu ....**Alt** + **V**

2. To display the Ruler, choose **Ruler** ....**R**

Save—Document/File

Saves the new document under a file name. Saves an existing document under the same file name.

Once you choose the File Save command, the current version of the document replaces the original.

Mouse Steps

1. Click on the File menu.

2. To save a document under the same file name, directory, and drive, click on the **Save** command.

TIP

Click on the **Save** button on the Standard toolbar as a shortcut for steps 1 and 2.

Keyboard Steps

1. Pull down the File menu .... **Alt** + **F**
2. To save the document under the same file name, directory, and drive, choose **Save** .... **S**

TIP

Use either of these shortcuts instead of steps 1 and 2: **Ctrl+S**.

Save As—Document/File

Saves the document under a different drive, directory, format, or name.

Mouse Steps

1. Click on the File menu.
2. Choose the Save **As** command.
3. Choose from the following variations:

To save	Click
Under a different drive	Drives list box
Under a different directory	Directories list box
Under a different name	File Name text box
In a different format list box	Save File as Type

4. To save, click on **OK**.

Keyboard Steps

TIP

Instead of steps 1 and 2 you can press **F12**.

1. Pull down the File menu .... `Alt` + `F`

2. Choose Save As .... `A`

3. Choose the variation under which you want to save the document:

To save	Press
Under a different drive (Drives list box) .... `Alt` + `V`	
Under a different directory (**Directories** list box) .... `Alt` + `D`	
Under a different name (File **Name** text box) .... `Alt` + `N`	

In a different format
(Save File as Type list box) .... [Alt] + [T]

4. To save, press .... [⏎]

Select—Text

Before you can move, format, delete, or change text or a graphic, you must first select the item you want to edit.

Mouse Steps

Item	To highlight
Any item or amount of text	Highlight (or drag) over the text you want to select.
A word	Double-click the word.
A graphic	Click the graphic.
A line of text	Click in the selection bar to the left of the line.
Multiple lines of text	Drag in the selection bar to the left of the lines.

Keyboard Steps

Item	To highlight, press
One character to the right	Shift + →
One character to the left	Shift + ←
To the end of the word	Ctrl + Shift + →
To the beginning of the word	Ctrl + Shift + ←
To the end of a line	Shift + End
To the beginning of a line	Shift + Home
One line down	Shift + ↓
One line up	Shift + ↑
To the end of a paragraph	Ctrl + Shift + ↓

Shortcut Menus—Select a Command

A shortcut menu is a menu that pops up to display the most common commands you use for the task you are trying to perform.

Mouse Steps

1. Do one of the following:

   Position the insertion point in the text or item you want to work with.

   Point to a location on a toolbar.

2. To open the menu, click the right mouse button.

3. Select the command you want.

To close the shortcut menu without choosing a command, click anywhere outside the menu.

Sort

Sorts the contents of a document by text, number, and date in ascending or descending order.

Mouse Steps

1. Select the text you want to sort.

Do not select any text if you want to sort the entire document.

2. Click on the Table menu.

3. Click on the Sort command.

4. Click on the **A**scending or **D**escending option button.

5. Click on the Type drop-down list box.

6. Click on **Text**, **Number**, or **Date**.

7. To begin sorting, click **OK**.

Keyboard Steps

1. Select the text you want to sort.

TIP

Do not select any text if you want to sort the entire document.

2. Pull down the Table menu .... `Alt` + `A`

3. Choose Sort .... `T`

4. Choose Ascending or
    Descending .... `Alt` + `A`

    or

    `Alt` + `D`

5. Pull down the Type list box .... `Alt` + `Y`

6. Select **Text**, **Number**, or **Date** .... `↑` or `↓`

EXAMPLE

To sort through a table of contents, choose **Text** in Ascending order. Your table of contents will be in alphabetical order starting from A and running through Z.

7. To begin sorting, press .... `↵`

Spell Check

Checks the selected text (from one word to the entire document, depending on your command) for spelling errors, including duplication of words based on its own dictionary. It also suggests the correct spelling for unmatched words.

Mouse Steps

1. Position the cursor at the beginning of the document to check the whole document from beginning to end. Or position the cursor where you want to begin checking for spelling errors. You can even select a single word.

2. Click on the **T**ools menu.

3. Click on the **S**pelling command.

TIP

Skip steps 1 and 2 by selecting the **Spelling** button on the Standard toolbar.

4. Look at the Not in Dictionary text box for the first word that is unmatched.

5. Choose one of the following options:

Ignore	Ignores suggestion and moves to the next un-matched word.
Ignore All	Ignores suggestion for every occurrence of that word and moves to the next unmatched word.
Change	Changes the word to its suggested spelling or the spelling you type in the Change to text box.

Change All	Changes every occurrence of that word to its suggested spelling or the spelling you type in the Change to text box.
Add	Adds the highlighted word to the dictionary.
Undo Last	Undoes or deletes the preceding correction.
Suggest	Suggests corrections in the suggestions box. Choose Change or Change All.
Close or Cancel	Stops the Spelling command.

6. If you started at the beginning instead of in the middle of the document, Word will not ask you "Do you want to continue checking at the beginning of the document?" If you forgot to start at the beginning, you can answer this question by clicking on Yes, No, or Help.

Keyboard Steps

1. Position the cursor at the beginning of the document to check the whole document from beginning to end. Or position the cursor where you

want to begin checking for
spelling errors. You can even
select a single word ....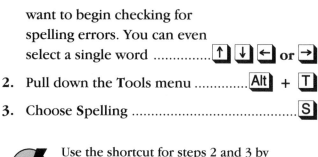

2. Pull down the Tools menu ....Alt + T

3. Choose Spelling ....S

Use the shortcut for steps 2 and 3 by
pressing **F7**.

TIP

4. Look at the Not in Dictionary text box for the
first word that is unmatched.

5. Choose one of the following options:

Ignore	Ignores suggestion and moves to the next unmatched word	Alt + I
Ignore All	Ignores suggestion for every occurrence of that word and moves to the next unmatched word	Alt + G
Change	Changes the word to its suggested spelling or the spelling you type in the Change to text box	Alt + C

Change All	Changes every occurrence of that word to its suggested spelling or the spelling you type in the Change to text box	`Alt` + `L`
Add	Adds the highlighted word to the dictionary	`Alt` + `A`
Undo Last	Undoes or deletes the preceding correction	`Alt` + `U`
Suggest	Suggests corrections in the suggestions box. Choose **Change** or **Change All**	`Alt` + `S`
Close or Cancel	Stops the Spelling command	`Esc`

6. If you started at the beginning instead of in the middle of the document, Word will not ask you "Do you want to continue checking at the beginning of the document?" If you forgot to start at the beginning, you can answer this question by choosing **Yes, No,** or **Help** .... `Y`, `N`, or `H`

Spike—Collect Text or Graphics

If you want to remove several items from one or more documents and place them elsewhere, use the Spike. Spike stores each item you delete. The first item you delete appears at the top of the Spike entry, the second follows.

This option can only be performed from the keyboard.

TIP

Keyboard Steps

1. Highlight the data (text and/or graphic) you want to store.

The more computer memory you have, the more you will be able to store using the Spike.

TIP

2. To move the text or graphic to the Spike, press ....**Ctrl** + **F3**

3. To continue adding text or graphics, repeat steps 1 and 2.

To view the contents in the Spike, from the **Edit** menu choose AutoText and select **Spike**.

TIP

Spike—Empty

Inserts the contents of the Spike and then empties itself.

TIP

This action can only be performed from the keyboard.

Keyboard Steps

1. Position the cursor where you want to insert the items you have grouped together in the Spike.

2. To insert all items stored and then empty the Spike, press .... Ctrl + Shift + F3

Spike—Insert

Inserts the contents of the Spike that you have grouped together.

TIP

This action can only be performed from the keyboard.

Keyboard Steps

1. Position the cursor where you want to insert the items you have grouped together in the Spike.

2. Type ....**Spike**

3. To insert all items grouped in the
   Spike, press ....[F3]

Standard Toolbar—Customize

*Creates a custom toolbar that contains the buttons
you use most often.*

Mouse Steps

1. Open the **View** menu.

2. Choose **T**oolbars.

3. Select the **N**ew button

4. In the **T**oolbar Name box, type a name for the
   new Standard toolbar.

5. In the **M**ake Toolbar Available To box, choose
   which documents in which to store the
   toolbar and choose **OK**.

6. Select the **T**oolbars tab.

7. In the **C**ategories box, select the category that
   contains the buttons you want to use.

8. Drag the button to the new toolbar.

9. When you are finished adding buttons, select
   Close.

Keyboard Steps

1. Select the View menu .... `Alt` + `V`

2. Choose Toolbar .... `T`

3. Select the New button .... `Alt` + `N`

4. In the Toolbar Name box, type a
   name for the new toolbar .... *name*

5. In the Make Toolbar Available To
   box, choose the documents in
   which to store the toolbar and
   press **Enter** .... `Alt` + `M`
   `↑` or `↓`

6. Choose **OK** .... `⏎`

7. Select the Toolbars tab .... `Alt` + `T`

8. In the Categories box, select
   the category that contains the
   buttons .... `Alt` + `C`
   `↑` or `↓`

9. Drag the button to the new toolbar.

10. When you are finished adding buttons,
    select Close .... `Tab`
    `⏎`

Style—Apply

A style is a group of formats that define the face of a document. Styles also form a cohesiveness that pulls your document together and makes it more readable.

Mouse Steps

1. Apply a singular style to your entire document by selecting the whole document. Apply a style to specific text by highlighting the text. Apply a style to a single paragraph by clicking anywhere in the paragraph.

2. Click on the Format menu.

3. Choose the Style command.

TIP

You can also click on the down arrow of the Style box on the Formatting toolbar, and then click on the desired style.

4. Click on a style from the Styles drop-down list box.

5. Apply the style and return to the document by clicking on the Apply button.

Keyboard Steps

1. Apply a singular style to your entire document by selecting the whole document. Apply a style to specific text by highlighting the text. Apply a style to a single paragraph by clicking anywhere in the paragraph.

2. Pull down the Format menu .... Alt + O

3. Choose Style .... S

4. Choose a style from the Styles
   drop-down list box .... Alt + S
   ↑ or ↓

5. Apply the style and return
   to the document by choosing
   Apply .... Alt + A

Style—Create

Documents are easier to read and understand when their styles are clearly defined. For example, for tips and examples in this book, we have created a style to distinguish them from the rest of the text. Every time your eyes see that particular style, you know there will be a tip or an example. As you create and revise styles, they are added to a style sheet. When you revise styles, they overwrite the old ones. To get more information on choosing options, see "Format—Character," "Format—Paragraph," or "Templates—Create."

Mouse Steps

1. Click on the Format menu.

2. Click on the Style command.

3. Click on the New button.

4. Type a style name in the Name text box.

If you want to revise an old style, choose it from the Based On list box by clicking on it.

5. Select **Format** to define a style by clicking on the options from the following list. Then click on **OK**.

Font

Paragraph

Tabs

Border

Language

Frame

Numbering

6. When you are finished setting the formatting style, click **OK** to close the dialog boxes.

7. To add the current options into a style and insert it on the style sheet, click on the **Apply** button.
OR
To revise a style with the current options and insert it into the style sheet, click on the **Modify** button.

Keyboard Steps

1. Pull down the Format menu ....⌐Alt⌐ + ⌐O⌐

2. Choose Style ....⌐S⌐

3. Choose New ....⌐Alt⌐ + ⌐N⌐

4. Type a style name in the Name text box ....*text*

TIP

If you want to revise an old style, choose it from the **B**ased On list box by pressing **Alt+B** and using the arrow keys to highlight it.

5. Select F**o**rmat to define a style and then choose from the following option buttons: .... **Alt** + **O**

Font .... **F**

Paragraph .... **P**

Tabs .... **T**

Border .... **B**

Language .... **L**

Frame .... **M**

Numbering .... **N**

6. When you are finished, close the dialog boxes .... ⏎
⏎

7. To add the current options into a style and insert it on the style sheet, choose **A**pply .... **Alt** + **A**
OR
To revise a current style with the current options and insert it into the style sheet, choose **M**odify .... **Alt** + **M**

Tab—Change

Sets and changes left, center, right, decimal, and dot leader tabs.

Mouse Steps

1. Position the cursor in the document where you want to set or change a tab. To set a tab for a whole paragraph(s), highlight it.

2. Click on the Format menu.

3. Click on the Tabs command.

4. Set new tabs by clicking on the Clear All button.

5. Type a new tab position in the Tab Stop Position text box or click on one from the list box.

6. From the Alignment section, click on one of the following options:

   Left

   Center

   Right

   Decimal

7. From the Leader section, click on one of the following options:

   1 None (no dot leaders)

   2 Dotted Line

   3 Dashed Line

   4 Solid Line

8. Click on the **S**et button.

9. To set additional tabs, repeat steps 5–8.

10. To confirm the tab settings and return to the document, click on **OK**.

Keyboard Steps

1. Position the cursor in the document where you want to set or change a tab. To set a tab for a whole paragraph(s), highlight it.

2. Pull down the F**o**rmat menu .... Alt + O

3. Choose **T**abs .... T

4. Set new tabs by choosing
   Clear **A**ll .... Alt + A

TIP

Delete a tab by typing the tab's position in the **T**ab Stop Position text box (press **Alt+T**). Then select the Cl**e**ar button or press (**Alt+E**).

5. Activate the **T**ab Stop Position
   text box .... Alt + T
   Type a new tab position or
   select one from the list box .... ↑ **or** ↓

6. From the Alignment section,
   choose one of the following:

   Left .... Alt + L

   Center .... Alt + C

   Right .... Alt + R

Decimal .... Alt + D

Bar .... Alt + B

7. From the Leader section,
    choose one of the following:

    1 None (no dot leaders) .... Alt + 1

    2 Dotted Line .... Alt + 2

    3 Dashed Line .... Alt + 3

    4 Solid Line .... Alt + 4

8. Choose Set .... Alt + S

9. To set additional tabs, repeat steps 5–8.

10. To confirm the tab settings and
    return to the document, press .... ⏎

Tab and Paragraph Marks— Display

Shows the tab and paragraph marks and other nonprinting characters in the document.

TIP

On the Standard toolbar, click on the **Show/Hide** (¶) button to display the nonprinting characters. To hide the marks, click on the **Show/Hide** (¶) button again.

Keyboard Steps

1. Pull down the Tools menu .... Alt + T

2. Choose Options .... O

3. On the View tab, choose any one or a combination of the following options from the Nonprinting Characters option box:

Tab Characters .... Alt + T

Spaces .... Alt + S

Paragraph Marks .... Alt + M

Optional Hyphens .... Alt + O

Hidden Text .... Alt + I

All.. Alt + A

TIP All these check boxes are toggles. If a check appears in the check box, the command is turned on. If you select the command again, you will turn it off.

4. To display or hide any of the nonprinting characters, press .... ⏎

Table—Calculations

Enables you to perform basic mathematical calculations in tables.

Mouse Steps

1. Position the insertion point in the cell in which you want the sum to appear.

2. Click on the Table menu.

3. Choose Formula.

4. Word analyzes and proposes the appropriate formula in the Formula box.

5. Choose **OK**.

Keyboard Steps

1. Position the insertion point in the cell in which you want the sum to appear.

2. Select the Table menu .... Alt + A

3. Choose Formula .... O

4. Word analyzes and proposes the appropriate formula in the Formula box.

5. Choose **OK** .... ⏎

Table—Create

Arranges data in a structure called a table that is organized by columns (vertical) and rows (horizontal). Using tables eliminates the need to use tabs throughout your document.

Mouse Steps

TIP

Create a table by clicking on the **Insert Table** button on the Standard toolbar. Drag the mouse over the grid to choose the number of rows and columns into which you want to arrange the table.

1. Position the cursor where you want the table inserted.

2. Click on the Table menu.

3. Click on the Insert Table command.

4. Type a number in the Number of Columns text box.

5. Click on the Number of Rows text box and enter a number.

6. To define the width of the columns, click on the Column Width text box and enter a number or select **Auto**.

7. To accept your choices, return to the document, and see the table in the document, click **OK**.

TIP

Fill in the table with your information by clicking in the cell into which you want to insert the information.

Keyboard Steps

1. Position the cursor where you want the table inserted.

2. Pull down the Table menu .... `Alt` + `A`

3. Choose Insert Table .... `I`

4. Type a number in the Number of Columns text box .... **#**

5. Activate the Number of Rows text box .... `Alt` + `R`
   Type a number in the text box .... **#**

2366.6.6.

66.6.66.

66.

6. To define the width of the columns, activate the Column Width text box .... <kbd>Alt</kbd> + <kbd>W</kbd>
   Type a number or select **Auto** .... **#** or <kbd>↑</kbd> <kbd>↓</kbd>

7. To accept your choices, return to the document, and see the table in the document, press .... <kbd>↵</kbd>

TIP Fill in the table with your information by pressing **Tab** to move from cell to cell horizontally. To begin a new row, press **Tab** from the end of the last row of the previous record.

Table—Edit

Edits the table by inserting or deleting a row or a column. For more information on tables see "Table—Create."

Mouse Steps

1. Select the cell where you want the new column to be inserted. (The selected column and all columns to its right will move one cell towards the right.)
   OR
   Select the cell where you want the new row to be inserted. (The selected row and all rows below it will move down one cell.)

2. Click on the Table menu.

3. Click on the **Insert Cells** command.

4. Click on the Insert Entire **C**olumn option.
   OR
   Click on the Insert Entire **R**ow option.

5. To insert a new column or row, click **OK**.

TIP

To delete a row or a column, highlight the column(s) or row(s) you want to delete and click on the Table menu. Click on the **D**elete Columns command or the **D**elete Rows command.

Keyboard Steps

1. Select the cell where you want the new column to be inserted. (The selected column and all columns to its right will move one cell towards the right.)
   OR
   Select the cell where you want the new row to be inserted. (The selected row and all rows below it will move down one cell.)

2. Pull down the Table menu .... Alt + A

3. Choose Insert Cells I

4. Choose Insert Entire **C**olumn .... Alt + C
   OR
   Choose Insert Entire **R**ow .... Alt + R

5. To insert a new column or
   row, press .... ↵

TIP

To delete a row or a column, highlight the column(s) or row(s) you want to delete, pull down the Table menu (press **Alt+A**), and choose **D**elete Columns (press **Alt+D**) or **D**elete Rows (press **Alt+D**).

Table—Split

Separates the table horizontally by creating a blank row above the current row. This feature can also be used to create a separate table.

EXAMPLE

Use this command to create sections in a table for emphasis by inserting space before and after a section.

Mouse Steps

1. Position the cursor where you want to split the table.

2. Click on the Table menu.

3. Click on the **S**plit Table command.

TIP

If you split the table in the wrong place, immediately click on the Undo button on the Standard toolbar. The sectioned table will be reverted to the previous table.

Keyboard Steps

1. Position the cursor where you want to split the table.

2. Pull down the Table menu .... Alt + A

3. Choose Split Table .... S

TIP

If you split the table in the wrong place, immediately pull down the Edit menu (press Alt+E) and select Undo Split Table (press U). The sectioned table will be reverted to the previous table.

Table Gridlines—Turn On

Displays a background that resembles graph paper and helps you position objects on a page on-screen. This command is used as a toggle to display or hide table gridlines.

Mouse Steps

1. Position the cursor anywhere in the table in which you want to display or hide the gridlines.

2. Click on the Table menu.

3. Click on the Gridlines command.

Keyboard Steps

1. Put the cursor anywhere in the table in which you want to display or hide the gridlines.

2. Pull down the Table menu .... Alt + A

3. Choose Gridlines L

Table of Contents—Compile

If you have applied built-in heading styles to headings, Word can use the heading styles to compile a table of contents. The table of contents tells the reader what major headings will be covered in the book and where to find them. To find minor headings and subjects, look in the Index. To create an index, see "Index—Create Entry" and "Index—Compile."

Mouse Steps

1. Format the headings you want to include with built-in heading styles.

2. Position the insertion point where you want to begin.

3. Click on the Insert menu.

4. Click on Index and Tables.

5. Select the Table of Contents tab.

6. **(Optional)** In the Formats box, select a format.

7. Choose **OK**.

Keyboard Steps

1. Format the headings you want to include with built-in heading styles.

2. Position the insertion point where you want to begin ..... $\boxed{\uparrow}$, $\boxed{\downarrow}$, $\boxed{\leftarrow}$ **or** $\boxed{\rightarrow}$

3.   Open the Insert menu .... Alt + I

4.   Select Index and Tables X

5.   Choose the Table of
     Contents tab .... Alt + C

5.   **(Optional)** In the Formats
     box, select a format .... Alt + T

6.   Press .... ⏎

If you are creating a table of contents from headings that aren't formatted with a built-in style, select the text and press **Alt+Shift+O**. When you're ready to compile, start with step 3.

Template—Create

Creates a pattern in which to organize a document. Standardizes types of documents you use often by including text, styles, AutoText entries, macros, and so on. For help defining the elements of the template, see "Macro—Record," "Macro—Assign to a Menu or to the Toolbar," or "Style—Create."

You can use this set of commands to create your own letterhead.

EXAMPLE

Mouse Steps

1.   Create the document you want to use as a template. (See "Style—Create" and "Macro—Record.")

2. Click on the File menu.

3. Click on Save **As**.

4. Under Save File as Type, choose **Document Template**.

5. In the File Name text box, name the template. Keep the .dot extension.

6. Click on **OK**.

Keyboard Steps

1. Create the document you want to use as a template. (See "Style—Create" and "Macro—Record.")

2. Open the File menu .... Alt + F

3. Choose Save **As** .... A

4. Under Save File as Type, choose **Document Template** .... Alt + T
   ↑ ↓

5. In the File Name text box, name the template. Keep the .dot extension .... Alt + N
   text

6. Choose **OK** .... ↵

Template—Use

Assigns a template to a document. If you don't choose a template, Word will automatically assign it the Normal template, which contains the standard settings.

Mouse Steps

1. Click on the **File** menu.
2. Click on the **New** command.
3. Click on a template from the **Template** list box.
4. To assign a template to a document, click **OK**.

Keyboard Steps

1. Pull down the **File** menu .... `Alt` + `F`
2. Choose **New** .... `N`
3. Activate the **Template** list box .... `Alt` + `T`
   Choose a template .... `↑` `↓`
4. To assign a template to a document, press .... `↵`

Text

See "Copy—Text," "Delete—Text," "Find and Replace—Text," "Paste—Text," or "Select—Text."

Thesaurus

Use the thesaurus to improve the precision and variety of your writing. You can find synonyms (words with the same meaning) for a selected word or phrase. In some instances, you may also find antonyms (words with opposite meanings).

Mouse Steps

1. In your document, highlight the word for which you want to find a synonym or antonym.

2. Click on the **Tools** menu.

3. Click on the **Thesaurus** command.

4. In the **Meanings** list box, choose a word that is closest to the meaning you want, or choose the Antonyms or Related Words options.

5. In the Replace with **S**ynonym text box, the word that is highlighted in the **Meanings** list box will appear. Choose a different word from the list box if you want.

6. **(Optional)** To look up synonyms or antonyms for the highlighted word, choose **L**ook Up.

7. **(Optional)** To go back to the previous word you looked up, choose the **P**revious button.

8. When the word you want is highlighted in the Replace with text box, choose the **R**eplace button.

Keyboard Steps

1. In your document, highlight the word for which you want to find a synonym or antonym.

2. Pull down the Tools menu .... 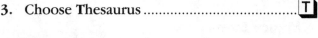 **Alt** + **T**

3. Choose Thesaurus .... **T**

Use the shortcut for steps 2 and 3: press **Shift+F7**.

TIP

4. In the Meanings list box, choose a word that is closest to the meaning you want, or choose the Antonyms or Related Words options .... **Alt** + **M**
   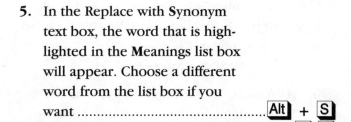 **↑** **↓**

5. In the Replace with Synonym text box, the word that is highlighted in the Meanings list box will appear. Choose a different word from the list box if you want .... **Alt** + **S**
   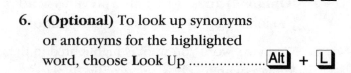 **↑** **↓**

6. **(Optional)** To look up synonyms or antonyms for the highlighted word, choose Look Up .... **Alt** + **L**

7. **(Optional)** To go back to
the previous word you looked
up, choose the **P**revious button ......`Alt` + `P`

8. When the word you want is highlighted
in the Replace with text box, choose the
Replace button ....`Alt` + `R`

Toolbar—Display

*A toolbar is a group of commonly used keys that the
user can quickly access with the mouse instead of
entering an entire series of commands one by one.
Word displays a toolbar at the top of the screen. Use
this command as a toggle to turn it on or off.*

Mouse Steps

1. Click on the **V**iew menu.

2. Click on the **T**oolbars command.

3. Click on the toolbar you want to turn on or off.

4. Click on **OK**.

Keyboard Steps

1. Pull down the **V**iew menu ....`Alt` + `V`

2. Choose **T**oolbars ....`T`

3. Select the toolbar you want to
turn on or off ....`↑` `↓`
`Space`

4. Select **OK** ....`⏎`

Toolbar Button—Delete

Use the mouse to delete a custom button from a toolbar.

Mouse Steps

1. With the toolbar you want to edit showing on-screen, click on the View menu.

2. Click on the Toolbars command.

3. Select Customize.

4. Drag the button off the toolbar to any other place.

5. To close the dialog box, click on the **Close** button.

Undo

Undoes the previous single command, format, or action.

TIP

To quickly undo a task, click the **Undo** button on the Standard toolbar.

Mouse Steps

1. Click on the Edit menu.

2. Click on the Undo command.

Keyboard Steps

1. Pull down the Edit menu .... Alt + E

2. Choose Undo .... U

TIP

Use the shortcut key combination **Ctrl+Z**.

View—Document

Word provides a variety of options concerning the viewing of documents. Choose one of the options below based on your specific task.

View	Displays	Select
Simplified layout and the default settings of the document	line spacing, font, point size	Normal
Structured format	heads, subheads, body text	Outline
Entire document	all formats of the text, headers, footers, footnotes	**Page Layout**
Single document and master document	body text	**Master Document**

View	Displays	Select
Enlarged or reduced		**Z**oom
Entire document	no rulers, toolbars and other screen elements	**Fu**ll Screen View
Entire document reduced	body text	**P**rint Preview

Mouse Steps

1. Click on the **V**iew menu.

2. Click on one of these options:

   Normal

   Outline

   Page Layout

   Master Document

   Zoom

Keyboard Steps

1. Pull down the View menu .... Alt + V

2. Choose one of the options from the preceding table by pressing the bolded letter ...... *selection letter*

Wizard

Use wizards to quickly lay out letters, memos, newsletters, or other common documents. Wizards take you step by step through the process of creating documents that are tailored to your preferences.

Mouse Steps

1. Click on the File menu.

2. Click on **New**.

3. Under New, select the **D**ocument option button.

4. In the **T**emplate box, select the wizard that you want to use and then choose **OK**.

5. Word displays a series of dialog boxes that take you through a step-by-step process. Follow the directions on the screen. Select the options you want.

6. Click on the **N**ext button to go to the next dialog box.

7. Choose **F**inish to close and begin filling in the text.

Keyboard Steps

1. Pull down the File menu .... **Alt** + **F**

2. Select New .... **N**

3. Under New, select the **D**ocument
    option button .... [Alt] + [D]

4. In the **T**emplate box, select
    the wizard that you want to
    use and then choose **OK** .... [Alt] + [T]
    [↑] or [↓]
    [↵]

5. Word displays a series of dialog boxes that
    take you through a step-by-step process.
    Follow the directions on the screen. Select
    the options you want.

6. Click on the **N**ext button to go
    to the next dialog box .... [Alt] + [N]

7. Choose **F**inish to close and
    begin filling in the text .... [Alt] + [F]
    [↑] or [↓]
    text

Word Count

*Counts the number of pages, words, characters,
paragraphs, and lines within a document.*

Mouse Steps

1. Click on the **T**ools menu.

2. Choose **W**ord Count.

3. Click on **Close** when you're finished looking
    at the statistics.

Keyboard Steps

1. Choose the Tools menu .... `Alt` + `T`

2. Select Word Count .... `W`

3. Select **Close** when you're
   finished looking at the
   statistics .... `↵`

Index